Embracing
Biological Humanism

Embracing Biological Humanism

Abandoning the Idea of God

NORMAN ORR

Archway Publishing books may be ordered through booksellers or by contacting:

Archway Publishing
1663 Liberty Drive
Bloomington, IN 47403
www.archwaypublishing.com
844-669-3957

ISBN: 978-1-4808-9869-1 (sc)
ISBN: 978-1-4808-9867-7 (hc)
ISBN: 978-1-4808-9868-4 (e)

Library of Congress Control Number: 2020921456

Print information available on the last page.

Archway Publishing rev. date: 1/28/2021

To all biological entities who read this book and
were encouraged and (or) strengthened,
and to all those who could not, did not, or would not.

Preface

Almost imperceptibly, the supposedly
supernatural is transformed into the natural.[1]

"Preposterous! How could you possibly even think about writing, much less actually write, a book recommending that humans abandon the idea of god—a concept that has existed, many would think, as long as humans have existed?" My wife tells me no one (she would be among them) will read this book. I'm expecting, however, that I can depend on a basic characteristic of human behavior, curiosity, to cause enough people to want to read the book to make my writing effort worthwhile.

A major background concept for this book is that we humans are largely unaware of who we actually are. Generally, we claim uniqueness in inappropriate ways. However, as you read, you are probably exercising a unique characteristic of humans. Other biological organisms communicate with one another, but as far as I am aware, no other biological organisms read. (But that's another book.)

A second major background concept arose from my recent reading of David Wootton's *The Invention of Science*. While Wootton doesn't directly explicate the concept of abandonment of obsolete ideas, his discussions demonstrate that acceptance of new ideas is completely dependent upon the abandonment of ideas that have become obsolete.

A third major concept arose from my watching a presentation by David Byrne at the Long Now Foundation titled "Good News and Sleeping Beauties." In the sleeping beauty section of the presentation, he discussed a number of ideas that had been presented, gained little recognition, and disappeared for a length of time, only to resurface later and gain significant acceptance.

Each of these major concepts will be demonstrated in my discussion of the reasons we need to abandon the idea of god.

I was born in 1935. Four years before I was born, Shailer Matthews published a book titled *The Growth of the Idea of God*. In a summarizing statement near the close of the book, he wrote the following:

> The idea of God is the outcome of the effort which men have made by the use of personal experience to gain help from those elements of the environment upon which they feel themselves dependent, and with which they attempt personal relations as instinctively as they breathe or protect their life.[2]

My premise for this book is that Matthews's view of the idea of god is a sleeping beauty whose time for awakening has arrived, and that to allow the idea to awaken, we as humans must abandon the long-held idea that we are created as special creatures by god and replace that concept with the premise that we are only biological organisms.

Those of you who have strong religious backgrounds will be thinking, *But what about the feeling that I have a personal relationship with god?* Matthews's statement, quoted above, acknowledges the importance of a feeling of a personal relationship. However, he had no recommendation other than the idea of god to fill that personal need. I am recommending that a thorough understanding of what it means to be a biological human organism allows one to embrace the concept of biological humanism to fill that need. A framework for biological humanism to function instead of a personal relationship with god will be presented.

One element of that framework is a proposed creed for biological humanists: "for the strength afforded by close association with other biological entities, we are truly grateful." I hope, and expect, that as you read further, you will experience a continuingly increasing appreciation for "the strength afforded by close association with other biological entities."

Contents

Chapter 1

God as an Idea

Major premise: All human cultural
artifacts are created by humans.
Minor premise: The idea of god is
a human cultural artifact.
Conclusion: The idea of god was
created by humans.[1]

Why, when, and how did humans create the idea of god?

Why Did Humans Create the Idea of God?

Information gained from four areas of academic study will help us answer these questions. Archaeology provides the foundation for much of the knowledge we have about early humans prior to the beginning of history.[2] Why are the findings of archaeologists important to us as humans? We humans are, both individually and as a species, who we have been. If we humans are to be able to understand who we currently are, including being able to answer the question "Why and when did humans create the idea of god?" we need to *really* know who we have been.

> The archaeologists job is to get through the object [what they dig up] to its maker; if he does that then, helped by the material qualities of the thing, he will begin to understand the society in which the thing's maker lived. Anybody can dig up things; but it is only by observation and interpretation that we can dig up the past.[3]

Archaeologists have amassed a tremendous amount of information about not only the physical structure of humans before history began at the advent of writing by humans, about 4,600 years ago,[4] but also about the living conditions of ancient humans. All of this information from archaeologists serves as a foundation for the information from other areas of academic study that will help us answer the questions about why and when humans created the idea of god.

Sociologists, building on the foundation of information from archaeology, have determined what the social life of early (prehistoric) humans must have been like. They lived in small bands, or groups of bands, and spent their time foraging for food. They had no permanent place of residence, establishing temporary resting places where food was plentiful. They migrated from location to location where the food supply was adequate for them. One can imagine their delight when they found a location in which food was relatively plentiful, adequate resting places were nearby, and they could feel a sense of satisfaction and appreciation. Since ritual (repetition of prescribed actions) is a common form of animal behavior,[5] early humans developed ritualistic actions as a way of expressing their feelings of appreciation to the unseen forces that made these accommodations available to them.

In time, they established traditional migration pathways

among the locations most profitable for them. Doubtless, they encountered other migrating bands, sometimes with which they had to compete for available resources. While somewhat disputed, significant evidence exists that cooperation is a biological imperative in animals, including humans.[6] Following this instinct, they discovered that by helping one another, their life conditions were improved.

Over time, the combination of their ritualistic activities and their sense of satisfaction and appreciation for the unseen forces that led to improvement in their life conditions gave birth to the concept of gods as providers of these favorable conditions. As they continued to include these gods in their community activities, the gods became personalized. "The gods ... were born of the habit of using the customs of social life to make the mysterious but controlling powers friendly persons."[7]

Why did humans create the idea of god? Humans created the idea of god as a way of explaining forces that were unknown but seemed to be helpful to them in their normal social lives.

The field of comparative religion adds an additional dimension to our search. Approaches to the study of comparative religion are diverse. Most of the classic textbooks in comparative religion include a section discussing similarities and differences within the major religions.[8] Most of the major religions include some concept of how god created the world. Some, including the Hebrew version in the Bible, indicate that the world was created by the spoken word of god. In theological terms, this concept is called *creation ex nihilo*—creation from nothing.[9] However, not all religions hold this view of god as creator. Swanson, in *The Birth of the Gods,* examines thirty different religions that claimed a creator/god.[10] The view of god as creator among these religions ranged from YHWH (Israelites) to a beetle (Lengua).

Barbroke Grubb was a missionary to the Lengua for about twenty years in the late 1800s.[11] His account of the Lengua's idea of creation is that the creator, in the guise of the beetle, sent forth from his hole in the earth a race of powerful beings who appear to have ruled the universe for a time. Afterward, the beetle formed man and woman from the clay that it threw up from its hole. The man and woman were joined together like Siamese twins. The pair was persecuted by the prior existing powerful beings and asked the creator to free them from their disadvantageous position. The creator separated them and gave them power to propagate so they might become numerous enough to withstand their enemies. Grubb points out that the Lengua's view of creation bears a remarkable resemblance to the Egyptian Scarabaeus and the ideas associated with it.

This brief examination of a small segment of information available through the study of comparative religions leads one to a conclusion that can be multiplied numerous times with a more thorough study, and that correlates directly with the conclusions reached through sociological studies: humans created the idea of god consistent with the physical and cultural circumstances in which they lived. The idea of god is a human cultural artifact.

When Did Humans Create the Idea of God?

Research in the area of anthropology, particularly anthropology of religion, helps us answer this question. According to Wallace, the earliest evidence of ritual of a religious kind among humans comes from between one hundred thousand and fifty thousand years ago. Archaeologists have discovered remains of bodies or parts of bodies of men and cave bears from somewhere in that range that appear to have been buried in ritualistic manner.[12] These ritualistic burials suggest belief in an afterlife, and therefore a god who could provide that afterlife.[13]

Because of a combination of the biological instinct for repetitive action and the feeling of appreciation and gratitude to unseen forces for the provision of food and shelter, prehistoric humans created the idea of god about fifty thousand years ago.

How Did Humans Create the Idea of God?

The answer to the *how* question consists of a restatement and restructuring of considerations in the questions of *why* and *when*.

a. The biological impulse for repetitive action in all biological organisms has been a part of animal life since it began. By the time Australopithecus developed (3.9 to 2.9 million years ago [YA]), the impulse for repetitive action would have been well established.

b. That impulse for repetitive action would have become formalized into ritualistic activity with the advent of language in humans. While the exact date of the development of language is unknown, it is suspected that language developed between the presence of Homo habilis (about 1.5 million YA) and the presence of Homo sapiens (about 300,000 YA).[14] In addition to performing ritualistic actions on the discovery of a bountiful food source, humans could now talk with one another about their good fortune and how that good fortune must have come about. Eventually, they began to give names to the various unseen forces, and a cadre of gods began to develop.

About 1,200 YA, human society rapidly (relative to prior time frames) began to become more complex. Toolmaking became more sophisticated, agriculture replaced gathering-hunting as the major food acquisition strategy, and localized areas of concentrated human populations (cities) began to develop.[15] This complex of cultural intensity would have had a significant influence on human thought about the gods.[16]

c. The concept of gods as the providers of eternal life appears to have developed about fifty thousand years ago, as indicated by the presence of ritualistic burials at that time. However, humans continued to think of gods in pluralistic terms at least as late as six thousand years ago, as evidenced in the Old Testament's emphasis on the importance of paying homage to only one god, Yahweh, as opposed to the other gods who still held the attention of most other cultures with whom the Hebrews were acquainted.* The Hebrew emphasis on only one god eventually prevailed, at least in the tradition of Western culture.

Because of their dependence on an innate biological inclination for motion and an urge to express their appreciation to the unknown forces that provided for their welfare, when language developed, humans created names for those unknown forces and called them gods. They named their gods in accordance with the cultural circumstances in which they found themselves and gave them characteristics that theoy deemed appropriate.

The concept that humans created the idea of god is not a recent one. Xenophanes (570–475 BCE) was a Greek philosopher, theologian, poet, and social religious critic.[17] He

* Interestingly, in the Old Testament account of the creation in the book of Genesis, two different words for god occur: one translates as *Yahweh*, the other as *Elohim*. Therefore, even as late as six thousand years ago, god was still considered a plurality, even among the Hebrews. While this information is generally known in academic biblical study, it is rarely known among lay religious people.

satirized traditional religious views of his time as human projections. In one of his poems he said this:

> But if cattle and horses and lions had hands,
> or could paint with their hands and create
> works such as men do, horses like horses and
> cattle like cattle also would depict the gods'
> shapes and make their bodies of such a sort
> as the form they themselves have.

This stanza represents the concept that humans not only created the idea of god but projected the idea they created from the context and circumstances in which they lived. The idea of god is a human cultural artifact, created by humans.

The concept that humans created the idea of god was a "sleeping beauty" that remained unconscious for more than two millennia, roused briefly in the early 1900s, and deserves a full awakening now.

Chapter 2

How Do We Know?

Realizing what you do *not* know is infinitely more informative that realizing what you *do* know.[1]

Those of you with a strong religious background are probably thinking, *You may say that humans created the idea of god, but I know better. I have a personal relationship with god.*

1. How Do You Know?

Do you believe in Santa Claus? Did you ever believe in Santa Claus? When did you begin to believe in Santa Claus? Why did you begin to believe in Santa Claus? If you no longer believe in Santa Claus, when and why did you stop believing in Santa Claus?

Do you believe in god? When did you begin to believe in god? Why did you begin to believe in god?

Santa Claus[2] is a mythical persona in Western culture. The image of Santa Claus, particularly in the United States and Canada, is significantly influenced by a poem, "A Visit from St. Nicholas," published in a newspaper in 1823 and accompanied by an illustration of St. Nicholas by Thomas

Nast. Clement Clark Moore claimed authorship of the poem in 1837.

Santa Claus is supposed to live at the North Pole. He seemingly has magical powers because he flies through the air in a sled filled with toys. The sled is pulled by flying reindeer. He reportedly keeps a list of the behavior of all the children in the world and rewards good children with gifts but leaves coal or switches for children with bad behavior. He delivers all those gifts to all those children all over the world on Christmas Eve and Christmas morning.

Why does Santa Claus live at the North Pole? When the story of Santa Claus was created, no historical record of anyone having visited the North Pole existed. A remote, unapproachable location helped to give credibility to the story of Santa Claus.

Consider the parallels in the story of Santa Claus and the story of god. At the time the two stories were created, each character represented lived in a remote, unapproachable location. Each had an unlimited knowledge of the behavior of earth's inhabitants. Each provided rewards for good behavior and less than desirable rewards for bad behavior. Each had powers beyond the reach of humans.

According to the premise of the research method *structural analogy*,[3] phenomena with similar structures have a common origin. Structural analogy suggests that, since the story of Santa Claus was created by humans as a cultural artifact, the story of god was also created by humans as a cultural artifact.

Consider again the questions at the beginning of the chapter: Do you believe in Santa Claus? Most adults would probably say that they do not believe in Santa Claus. Did you ever believe in Santa Claus? Almost everyone would probably say that they did at some time believe in Santa Claus. To the question, "When did you begin to believe in

Santa Claus?" most of us probably don't remember when we began to believe in Santa Claus. However, you probably don't think you were born believing in Santa Claus. You probably don't remember at what age you stopped believing in Santa Claus. However, most people remember that they stopped believing in Santa Claus when a friend or relative whom they trusted told them that Santa Claus was not real.

You were not born believing in Santa Claus. You believed in Santa Claus because people you trusted told you Santa Claus was real. You stopped believing in Santa Claus because people you trusted told you Santa Claus was not real.

Do you believe in god? Many, possibly most, of you will say you do believe in god. Have you ever believed in god? Many more will probably say that at some time they believed in god. Did you believe in god when you were born? Probably most would say they did not believe in god when they were born. When did you begin to believe in god? Although most won't be able to pinpoint a precise time when they began to believe in god, most would acknowledge that they began to believe in god when encouraged by someone whom they trusted who convinced them that they should believe in god.

You did not believe in god when you were born. You began believing in god when someone you trusted told you that you should believe in god. You continue to believe in god because no one you trust has told you that god is not real and you should not believe in him—and because you feel you have a personal relationship with him.

If Santa Claus and the idea of god are both cultural artifacts created by humans, how do you know that feeling is real?

2. *How Do We Know—Anything?*

You have to be carefully taught.[4]

A few years ago, I bought a print of a painting by René Magritte,[5] painted in 1929, and hung it on my kitchen wall. The painting is a reproduction of a briar pipe. The caption beneath the image says, "Ceci n'est pas une pipe"; this is not a pipe. I bought the print because I thought I understood what Magritte meant: the painting was not a pipe but an image of a device we humans call a pipe.[6*] In the process of preparing the print for hanging, I realized that the painting meant much more than what I had initially thought. Because of my increased understanding of the meaning of the painting, I searched for, and finally located, a briar pipe almost identical to the one in the painting. I had the pipe framed in a shadowbox, and beneath the pipe, I placed the caption, "N'est pas cici une pipe?": Is this a pipe? Soon thereafter, I located a small section of PVC water pipe and had it placed in a shadowbox with the caption, "Is this a pipe?"

I use this display to engage friends in conversation about how we know. When I ask why they think Magritte said it was not a pipe, they frequently say something like, "It looks like a pipe," and sometimes also indicate that it looks like the real pipe in the shadowbox. When I ask about the section of PVC pipe in the other shadowbox, they usually say that it is

* Pipe: *Webster's Collegiate Dictionary* says that the original meaning of the word *pipe* from the Latin meant to peep or make a sound. The first definition given is a tubular musical instrument; the second is a long, tubular instrument for conducting a liquid or gaseous substance. A device for smoking is the fifth definition given. Dictionary.com gives twenty-eight examples for using the word *pipe*, beginning with noun usage, followed by verb and so on. As with everything we know, meaning is determined by societal consensus in accordance with the cultural circumstances of the time.

also a pipe. When I ask whether the two pipes look like each other, they usually say they do not but that they are both pipes. Eventually, we are able to agree that we only know that each item is a pipe because we have been told by people we know and trust that they are pipes. Then I suggest that the same is true for everything else we know: we have to be carefully taught—about everything.

3. Social Constructionism

> It is through the daily interactions between people in the course of social life that our versions of knowledge become fabricated.[7]

Epistemology,[8] the study of how we know, was for centuries considered a component of the field of philosophy (as were many other fields of learning). Names like Socrates, Plato, Aristotle, Hume, Kant, Locke, and Descartes are associated with attempts to understand how we know. Numerous volumes have been written about the topic. No one's opinions seemed entirely satisfactory. However, it was Descartes's dictum, "I think, therefore I am," that for about five hundred years has appeared to be the predominantly accepted view of how we know—we simply think about something and know its validity.

Unfortunately, as the title of one of Damasio's[9] books indicates, Descartes's assumptions about human behavior were incorrect (more about that later). However, because of Descartes's influence, at least in Western society, we have concluded that we only need to think about something to know that what we think is truc.

The concept of social constructionism[10] had been hinted at in the field of sociology for a time, but it was not until

1966 when Berger and Luckmann published *The Social Construction of Reality*[11] that social constructionism began to be seriously considered as the means by which we humans know. Because of the importance of the question of how we know, both historically and currently, and because of the significance of the insights that social constructionism brings to the question, research and publication in the field of social constructionism[12] has become extensive and complex. However, at its core, the concept is rather simple but very profound: we humans create knowledge through our social interaction with one another and exercise our ability to accept as valid and assimilate the effects of that knowledge in our lives.

Summary

Think back to the basis for the claim in chapter 1 that humans created the idea of god. The sources from archaeology, anthropology, and sociology all claimed that the idea of god arose among humans because of their social interactions related to the circumstances in which they found themselves. Why did these writers not claim that the idea of god was socially constructed? If you noticed the publication dates of those authors, you will remember that they all reached their conclusions before 1966, when the concept of social construction began to gain general acceptance. Since what we know as a society "must be carefully taught," when the concept of social constructionism becomes generalized in society, acceptance of the reality that god is an idea that was socially constructed will be accepted and carefully taught.

Afterword

Those of you with strong religious convictions—if you're still with us—must assuredly be still thinking, *But what about the feeling that I have a personal relationship with god?* Please consider that not only were you carefully taught that god is real, you were also carefully taught that you should have a personal relationship with him. But please keep reading. More about feelings later.

Chapter 3

Mistaken, Misled, Misinformed, Uninformed

During the first 12 billion years until the emergence of Homo sapiens, it was not meaningful to think of man in God's image, or of a transcendent God interacting with man.[1]

"Who are you? said the caterpillar."[2]

"Who *ARE* you?"[3]

Background

Since humans created the idea of god, they also created the idea that god created humans. If we humans are not beings created by god, who are we?

How and why have humans erroneously believed for thousands of years that they were created by god?

Interestingly, the answer to each question is essentially the same. However, the details of the answer are so entangled that a strictly linear, reductionist approach to the answer is neither possible nor sufficient. I will attempt to present the answer in as straightforward a manner as possible.

However, be aware that in discussing emergent ideas, some circularity is necessary.

Humans are, according to currently accepted scientific concepts at this stage of existing human culture, an emergent biological species called Homo sapiens. The human biological organism is an emergent, nonlinear, complex system, which is alive. Life, however, "is a kind of behavior, not a kind of stuff."[4] It will be through an examination of a variety of human behaviors, and the rationale for those behaviors as explicated by current understandings in neuroscience, that we shall be able to answer the question in the second epigram at the beginning of the chapter. Our understanding of those behaviors should also help us in our understanding of the question, Who are we? However, a basic understanding of who we are is necessary before we begin to examine our behavior.

A. Who Are We?

"Keep it simple, stupid."[5]

Human, n. A gut that can talk.[6*]

I suggested in chapter 1 that we humans are who we have been. At a surface level, we seem to be more than passingly interested in who we have been, as evidenced by the success of numerous enterprises designed to help us discover our genealogical backgrounds. That interest, however, betrays

---

* *Webster's Seventh New Collegiate Dictionary* defines human as: "of, relating to, or characteristic of man; being a man; having human form or attributes"—hardly an informative definition of who we as humans actually are. While my definition may be a bit shocking initially, as we consider it further, I expect that my choice of that definition will become clear.

a bit of a shortsighted view of who we have been. Our true ancestry dates back not a few hundreds, or even thousands of years, but billions of years—about four billion years.[7] As E. O. Wilson aptly put it, "there they are, buried within the cells of each of us, those original strands of DNA."[8] Our genealogy begins when life began on earth. Since god didn't create us, we emerged as life emerged—and everything we can know about any life form tells us something about ourselves.

Have you ever asked yourself why you were born in an aquatic environment? (Possibly some of you don't know that you were born in an aquatic environment.) Why, because fish are a part of our ancestry, and we haven't seen the need to, or been able to, change that part of our development. If that sounds totally off the wall to you, you owe it to yourself to read Neil Shubin's *Your Inner Fish.*[9]

But, back to my definition of human. Have you ever read any vertebrate embryology?[10] The description of the first few minutes following the fertilization of the egg of a vertebrate (which includes humans) is highly informative. The description centers on motion.[11] Sperm moves to the location of the egg and penetrates the exterior of the egg. The egg immediately begins to divide, and as the cells multiply, they begin to form a line, known as the primitive gut line. As the cells in the gut line mature, they begin to migrate to various locations at which the major organs of the body will develop. Every organ in the human body, except the brain, develops from the initial cells of the primitive gut line. In a few days, a line of cells, called the neural crest, develops. The brain develops from that line of cells. The vertebrate body is initially a gut. The brain is an add-on.

The vertebrate gut contains a complete and independently operating nervous system, the enteric nervous system.* Guts have been performing life-sustaining activities for animals at least since worms appeared on earth, eons before the appearance of brains in the sense in which we think of our brains. The discovery of the enteric nervous system was first made popular by a book titled *The Second Brain.*[12] This book serves as an excellent example for transition to our next subject of consideration—biases.

Biases

When considered thoroughly and seriously, the title of that book should have been *The First Brain,* since from an embryological perspective, the gut line precedes the development of the neural crest. Also, guts have been a functional organ much longer than brains. Why then did the author call the enteric nervous system the second brain? The obvious answer, at least to me, is social bias. As we will consider more extensively later, we humans have been misled to believe that the brain is the most important organ in the human body. The author of *The Second Brain* was obviously influenced by that long-standing social bias and either could not or would not allow himself to refer to the enteric nervous system as the first brain, in spite of all the evidence to the contrary. This example illustrates the significance that social biases have in affecting our lives. Curiously, those social biases result from usually normal (but sometimes abnormal) functioning in the brain.

---

* Some connections do exist between the brain and the enteric nervous system; however, those connections exist simply for the exchange of information between the brain and the gut. The functional activities of the gut are under the complete control of the enteric nervous system.

B. How and Why Have Humans Erroneously Believed for Thousands of Years That They Were Created by God?

> "Let me tell you about how our brain is built, how it makes mistakes, how it gets things done for us, and *how we put a spin on it* [emphasis added] that makes it all seem like we are personally in charge."[13]

The brain operates normally on the basis of biases.[14]* ** Our emotional lives depend on this operational premise.

In a thoughtful, sweeping study of the importance of biological rhythms,[16] the authors say,

---

* The word *bias* is itself a victim of the phenomenon of cultural biases we are currently considering. In *Webster's Seventh New Collegiate Dictionary*, the first definition of bias is "a line diagonal to the grain of the fabric"; the second definition is "an inclination of temperament or outlook; especially prejudice." In dictionary.com,[15] words related to *bias* include "intolerance, favoritism, tilt, bigotry, prejudice, preference, leaning, unfairness, tendency, inclination, sway, slant, distort, incline, penchant, bent, predisposition." The origin of *bias* is reported as middle French—oblique. As used in research in neuroscience, the meaning of "bias" is an inclination based on a bodily response, not a culturally induced prejudice, which is the predominant meaning we have come to use and depend on.

** This concept is itself a kind of "sleeping beauty" idea (remember this concept from the preface?). Most of the supporting evidence for this premise bears a relatively recent publication date. However, the premise was suggested at least as early as 1973 by John Bowlby,[17] who wrote, "It seems more probable that *a baby arrives in this world with certain built-in biases,* one of which is to look at a human face in preference to other objects." Unfortunately, because of our cultural bias in favor of the *thinking* brain over the reality of the prominence of the *feeling* body (more about this later), Bowlby has never been given the serious consideration he deserves, even by the psychiatric community of which he was a part. His concepts are barely mentioned, even in DSM-V.

> Whether suddenly alarmed or chronically anxious, whether temporarily comforted or steadily confident, the way a man, or woman thinks and feels is determined in significant degree by the strong *genetic biases* [emphasis added] to respond unthinkingly to the natural clues [to potential danger and danger situations unique to the adaptive environment of the species.])

We and our mutual biological counterparts have survived ever since brains were developed because brains learned to operate on the premise of biases.

Brain biases are not limited to responses to emotional or dangerous situations, as important as those are. In a study of brain activity about visual perception, the authors[18] found that even when we are not actively looking at something, "there are inherent biases in cortical dynamics" that allow us to integrate our perception of images and brightness to more readily comprehend the nature of the object being viewed. They further suggest that such inherent biases indicate that they work in a fashion that is unadulterated by the effects of sensory stimulation, attention, or working memory (i.e., they work all on their own). The brain operates on the principle of biases to be able to function efficiently. Efficiency is a primary principle of biological survival; survival is a primary principle of living organisms. The brain developed to help biological organisms survive. It operates on the basis of biases to aid in the survival of the organism of which it is a part.

Joseph LeDoux traces, in detail, the four-billion-year development of modern human brains, beginning with either a community of early cells or an actual cell or cell type (which appeared between 4 billion and 3.8 billion YA, about half a billion years after the earth was formed)[19] to the presence of functioning, modern human brains about fifty thousand years ago. You may be thinking, *What does a collection of cells have to do with the human brain?* LeDoux summarizes the answer this way: survival strategies were built into ancient single-cell organisms, continued when multicellular life forms developed, taken over by neurons when they developed in early invertebrates, passed on to vertebrates when they developed and subsequently used by humans and all other animals, regardless of the simplicity or complexity of their bodies.[20] We inherited the basic structures for our brains from those original cells, and through time and experience, our brains developed.

At least as early as the presence of bacteria (3.5 BYA) life forms had to obtain nutrients and avoid danger. Through experience, they learned to distinguish the difference between beneficial and dangerous situations and began to be able to respond positively to the beneficial ones and negatively to the dangerous ones. The responses became automatic—reflective. By about 3 BYA, organisms began to become more complex, and the first unicellular organisms developed about 2 BYA. The reflective responses, called *fixed reaction patterns*,[21] of these organisms began to develop into patterns of behavior in response to the circumstances of their environment. Over time, these fixed reaction patterns developd as sequences of behavior.

By about 900 MYA when plants first developed, and 800 MYA when sponges* (the first complex animal life forms) developed, this fixed reaction pattern activity was well established in biological life forms. Plants bend to reach the

* Sponges were the first complex animal organism with a hollow body cavity—the precursor of the gut. Jellyfish, which appeared about 700 MYA, contained the first neurons. Accordingly, the enteric nervous system began to develop between 800 and 700 MYA.

sunlight, birds scatter at the sound of a loud explosion, and you duck when something unexpected touches the top of your head because of reaction pattern activity. As LeDoux says, "the roots of behaviors that animals routinely call upon in day-to-day life are more ancient than we generally acknowledge."[22] Now, back to biases in our brains. Through all those billions of years before animals developed brains, life forms (which depended on fixed reaction patterns and from which brains developed) established patterns of behavior that supported survival. Those behaviors that were most successful were favored, and those that were less successful were ignored. The pattern of bias toward successful behavior was instilled in successful life forms; that pattern of bias was carried forward as the brain developed and still continues today.

Confabulation

Think again about the circumstances in which early humans lived and in which they created the idea of god. They invented the best idea they could think of, but they were mistaken, and even in early human culture, their ideas, including the mistaken ones, were carefully taught—for generations and generations.

What is it about humans that allow us to create ideas and sustain them through countless generations, only later to discover that the ideas were mistakes? Only recently, with the advent of neuroscience, have we been able to find an answer to those questions. Some of the answers are found in what is currently considered abnormalities in human thought and behavior. One such abnormality is called confabulation.

Confabulation[23] is a recently (early 1900s) explicated phenomenon of human behavior, originally designated as a memory distortion. However, significant evidence exists that indicates that confabulation, as with biases, is an ancient and very complex phenomenon. The nature of confabulation can possibly be best demonstrated with a simple example: Suppose someone is asked a question to which they do not know the answer. Instead of saying that they do not know the answer, they make up an answer that, to an observer, on its face, does not seem at all feasible. However, when questioned whether the person is sure of the answer, they insist that the answer is correct. That is confabulation.

Our brains developed to help us solve problems that favor our survival. When we are in a situation in which we do not know what to do, our brains propose solutions for us. Part of our brains assess the feasibility of the solutions, and we try to pick the solution that is most advantageous for us. These activities take place in the frontal lobes, possibly specifically the orbitofrontal lobes.[24] Hirstein describes a number of cases in which damage to the orbitofrontal lobes produces unusual and sometimes even bizarre behavior. Apparently, damage to certain areas of the orbitofrontal lobes reduces our ability to properly assess the accuracy of our proposed thoughts and actions. In some of those situations, our brain confabulates a solution and we act on the confabulation without being aware that it is disadvantageous to us. Confabulation in those circumstances is considered a pathology.

However, not all confabulation is pathological.[25] Novelists' ability to invent interesting, and sometimes even gripping, stories is dependent on the brain structures that provide confabulation. Daydreaming can be a very relaxing result of confabulation. Science fiction is strongly dependent on our capacity for confabulation. As long as the judgmental capacity of our brains is in effect, our ability for confabulation is a positive factor.

Our capacity for confabulation, as with our capacity for bias, has been a part of our brains for eons. When our ancestors, about fifty thousand years ago, confabulated the idea of god, they had no circumstances to suggest that their ideas were incorrect. The confabulation seemed correct, a bias developed in favor of that confabulation, the confabulation was carefully taught, so that today, approximately 78 percent of the human population believes and acts on that confabulation. That's the spin we put on it that makes us think that god is in charge.

Mistaken

We are mistaken about our belief in god because our ancestors were mistaken in their confabulation about the source of the provision of circumstances that were favorable to them. We are also mistaken in continuing to propagate their mistake when we have sufficient evidence that their confabulation was just that—a confabulation and not an accurate description of the circumstances of our life on earth.

What difference does it make? If we humans have been content for fifty thousand years believing that god actually exists and that we are special beings created by god, why shouldn't we just continue on our merry way? One reason is that to pretend we are something other than what we actually are makes us imposters (but that's another book). More to the point here, unless we acknowledge the mistake confabulated by our ancient ancestors, and continued by us since then, we will never be able to accurately answer the question at the beginning of the chapter, "Who are you?" Nor will we be able to fully understand our behavioral responsibilities unless we understand and acknowledge fully that we are emergent biological beings rather than special creatures created by god.

The mistake implied in the title of a popular gospel song, "God Will Take Care of You," helps demonstrate this point. Fully recognizing that we are emergent biological beings requires us to acknowledge that we are responsible for our own welfare and not dependent on god to take care of us. We partially acknowledge that personal responsibility anytime we seek professional medical advice. Modern medical practice, to a large degree, is dependent on the realization that we are, as humans, emergent biological beings. Most medical practices and medical products are developed through experimentation with animals, to a large extent, mice, before they are approved for medical use for humans. That practice would not exist were it not for a socially accepted concept (although rarely consciously stated) that humans are emergent biological beings.

Numerous examples of unconscious behavior such as this one could be given. We need to become aware of the subconscious behaviors so we can consciously acknowledge who we actually are, admit the mistakes of our ancestors that we continue to support, and reap the full benefit of that acknowledgment.

Misled

Misled[26] is defined as "to lead in a wrong direction or into a mistaken action or belief; synonym, see DECIEVE." That definition implies a strictly culturally developed concept to the term that suggests ill intent on the part of an actor. While I am not aware of any direct consideration that suggests that misleading may be a biologically induced activity, I am aware of some evidence that suggests it may be. It is possible that misleading may be a long-standing biological technique supporting survival.

Careful observers of the behavior of chimpanzees[27] have found that, in most circumstances, chimpanzees willingly share food items that they discover. However, if a troop discovers a food source in which some elements are particularly rich in nutrients, some individuals have been known to hide those elements to save them for later, individual consumption. It seems to me that it would be a stretch to think that those chimpanzees consciously intended to mislead the rest of the troop so as to be able to consume those nutrient-rich elements. It seems more likely that an innate, biological imperative for survival led them to their actions.

If the general rule for chimpanzee feeding behavior is mutual sharing, were those chimpanzees that hid choice food elements misleading the rest of the troop? Yes. Was the hiding activity conscious? Probably not, in the sense that we consider consciousness. More likely, it was an innate, biological survival technique. If my premise is correct, that behavior did not originate with chimpanzees; it was inherited genetically from prior biological ancestors. The activity of *misleading* and being *misled* probably is not, as our current definition implies, solely a culturally developed activity. Rather, it is probably a long-standing, biologically induced survival technique that we fail to recognize because of our mistaken understanding of who we are as humans and that we mistakenly characterize because of our misunderstanding.

What difference does it make whether our propensity to be misled and to mislead results from an innate biological imperative or from a culturally developed concept? As we continue to consider what it means for us to have been misled, we need to be able to determine not only *that* the activity occurred but why the activity occurred and continued to exist for extended periods of time without our being aware of it.

Determining exactly when we moved from *misleading* as a fixed reaction pattern activity to a conscious activity is impossible to determine. However, the oldest known, almost complete legal code[28*] discovered is the code of Ur-Nammu. The content of that code suggests that some of the behavior covered by the code would have been misleading behavior. Apparently, for at least four thousand years, we have been consciously, in some circumstances, misleading others—and accordingly, being misled.

What's the relationship between our propensity to mislead and be misled and our propensity to believe in god? Belief in god led us to believe that we were special creatures created for god's pleasure rather than being emergent biological beings. That mistaken belief has allowed us to conceal from ourselves who we actually are. Anyone, past or present, who supports or has supported that concept of humans is being, and has been, misled.

Misinformed

Our ability to be misled sometimes, maybe even frequently, causes us to be misinformed. To investigate this phenomenon requires a consideration of what it means to believe. To believe is defined as "to have confidence in the truth, the existence, or the reliability of something, although without absolute proof that one is right in doing so."[29] In the context that we are considering, a belief is a mistaken bias that is superimposed by a culturally accepted authoritative

* Ur-Nammu's reign was from 2112 to 2095 BCE. Fragments of legal codes about one hundred years earlier have been found, but this is the oldest, extant, almost complete legal code.

entity upon a human society that is misled, misinformed, and uninformed.

Consider an idea that fits this definition. Almost everyone is familiar with Descartes's famous phrase, "I think, therefore I am." Without the prevailing cultural influence of belief that humans are a special creation of god, fostered for centuries by the authority of religious church hierarchies, Descartes probably would not have reached that conclusion. However, because of the prevailing cultural bias favoring that position, that phrase and the concept it presents of humans has been, and continues to be, the prevailing concept of what it means to be human—our ability to think makes us who we are.

At the risk of being possibly a bit anachronistic,* Descartes could not have been more wrong. Experimental evidence exists[30] which shows that action precedes thought. In an experiment, participants were fitted with a timing mechanism that would register brain responses following an action that the participant was asked to perform. The portion of the brain responsible for *producing* an action fired before the portion of the brain *recognizing the performance* of the action. We act, and then we think. Damasio's[31] view, stated briefly, is "for us then, in the beginning was being, and only later was it thinking. ... We are, and then we think ..."

Likely not entirely, but certainly to a great extent, current support for the popular dictum "mind over matter" results from Descartes's influence. In this instance, human society was misinformed and believed the misinformation because a culturally accepted authoritative entity proposed and supported the idea.

* Possibly, some of the supporting evidence of the ideas for Descartes's error would not have been possible for him to know at the time. That, however, does not excuse the extent of his error and its subsequent influence.

Belief in god follows a similar pattern. Our ancient ancestors confabulated the idea of god; that idea became culturally acceptable and eventually was supported and fostered by culturally accepted authoritative entities; was carefully taught to support and assure its continuation; and was assisted in its endurance by occasional, if not frequent, misinformation. That combination of circumstances helps prevent us from understanding and acknowledging who we actually are as humans.

Uninformed

How can I say that we are uninformed when we live in the age of twenty-four-hour television broadcasts and Wikipedia; higher percentages of the populations of most countries have at least high school education, larger percentages of people have college degrees and advanced degrees, and so on? Granted, we have access to more information than we can possibly manage. However, unfortunately, that does not mean that we are well informed. We are possibly somewhat informed about topics that are of interest to us, but what about those topics that do not interest us? Simply because we are not interested does not mean that they are unimportant to us. How many of you have read more than five of the books in the bibliography of this book? I'm not intending to embarrass you, and certainly not to berate you. I'm simply trying to make a point; as a society, we are generally uninformed about who we actually are as humans. Generally, we take it for granted that we know who we are and don't need to be concerned about what we *don't* know about who we are. However, take a moment to look again at the epigrams at the beginning of chapter 2.

Much of the recent blame for our being uninformed

results from our extreme dependence on reductionism.[32] While reductionism has allowed great understanding of many aspects of human existence, including much of the information provided in this book, particularly about how the brain operates, the approach of reductionism generally has so separated fields of learning and experimentation that very little cross-understanding exists even among highly educated people. To fully understand who we are as humans, we need details. However, we also need cross-pollination to be able to know and understand who we actually are. As Stephen Rose suggests, "We require epistemological diversity ... to be able to know and understand the ontological unity of our world"[33]: without an extensive knowledge of all aspects of life, we will never be able to understand who we actually are.

To refer again to the two questions at the beginning of the chapter: 1) "Who are you?" You are an emergent, complex biological organism with a genealogical heritage that goes back to the beginning of time. You are not a special being created by an idea (god) confabulated by human ancestors about fifty thousand years ago.

2. "Who ARE you?" I am the person who is attempting to help you answer question number one.

Chapter 4

God: An Idea Whose Time Has Passed

Plenty of [ideas][*] which we now regard as plain wrong have been successful in the past.[1]

The times, they are a-changing.
—Bob Dylan

How will humans be able to abandon the idea of god? Reluctantly and grudgingly. Because of our penchant for depending on brain biases, we have a long history of continuing to depend on ideas and patterns of action long after they have ceased to be beneficial. We'll consider some of those ideas that we have clung to tenaciously and then abandoned.

---

[*] Wooton's actual word was *theories*. The second definition[2] of *theory* is "a proposed explanation whose status is still conjectural ...." *Idea* is defined as "any conception in the mind as a result of mental understanding, awareness, or activity." I do not think Wooton would object to the substitution of the word *idea* in his statement about theories.

Gathering-Hunting as a Means of Livelihood*

About twelve to eleven thousand years ago, humans invented agriculture as a primary means of livelihood. The invention had a tremendous effect on the cultural and social life of humans.[3] Agriculture allowed the concentration of populations and the subsequent development of cities. Some[4] consider agriculture, particularly the plow, to be the source of monogamy, a phenomenon that many claim as a requirement by god. Gathering-hunting was largely abandoned as a means of livelihood, except in areas of the world where technology was not advanced. That abandonment had profitable results for humanity.

The Earth Is Flat

The flat earth idea demonstrates a number of phenomena associated with the concept of human abandonment of ideas that are out of date. One can easily imagine that early humans thought the earth was flat. By the time language developed, humans had already moved onto areas of the earth where savannas and plains dominated the landscape. Perceptually, in those settings, the earth does appear flat. Any discussion they may have had about the appearance of the earth most assuredly would have been consistent with their perceptions.

The premise that ancient Asian cultures believed in a flat earth[5] derives from archaeological recovery of religious writings indicating that the earth was a flat disk floating upon water. Early Norse and Germanic writers indicated a

* Recall my note about the arrangement of this term in chapter 1. I also contend that while we have largely abandoned this practice physically, we still, some more than others, cling to it psychologically. However, that's a topic to be considered elsewhere.

similar belief. In China, that concept remained until contact with Jesuit missionaries in the seventeenth century.

In Western culture, from the time of Socrates forward,[6] most philosophers and astronomers believed the earth was a sphere. Roundness of the earth was central to Aristotle's cosmology and was assumed in a measurement of the Earth's circumference in the third century BCE. Even during the so-called Dark Ages of the medieval period, virtually all scholars believed in a round earth.

However, somewhere between 1860 and 1890, a myth developed and was promulgated, claiming that during the medieval period, everyone believed the earth was flat. The author of that myth wanted to claim that belief in a flat earth was required as a belief in a biblical view of the earth as created by god.

Similarly, occasionally organizations still occur in support of belief in a flat earth. The flat earth society was formed in Dover, United Kingdom, in 1956. In 1972, a follower in that organization, in California, increased the organizations' membership to about three thousand. The society declined in the 1990s but was revived as a website in 2004. Members of the flat earth society and other similar organizations claim that NASA and other government agencies conspire to delude the public into believing the earth is a sphere. They claim that NASA photoshops satellite images to present the earth as a sphere and that that activity is known by only a highly select number of individuals.

This brief review of the idea of the earth as flat presents a number of concepts associated with the human practice of inventing and then abandoning ideas. First, most ideas, in some fashion, originate from and depend on human perception. Second, ideas usually prevail as long as those perceptions are not questioned. Third, when perceptions are questioned and the questioning is supported by substantial evidence, which gains adequate social acceptance, the outdated ideas are usually abandoned, frequently, if not largely, to the benefit of human society as a whole. Fourth, if the abandoned ideas return and gain some acceptance, the new acceptance is usually based on biases held by a minor portion of the human population, usually largely to the deficit of human society as a whole. These criteria will be used later in an assessment of the concept of abandoning the idea of god.

The Earth Is the Center of the Universe[7]

The idea of the earth as the center of the universe was popularized by the philosopher Aristotle in the fourth century BCE (before Christian era) in his concept that the universe was a series of concentric circles. The earth was at the center of those concentric circles. Earth was surrounded by water, water surrounded by air, and air surrounded by fire—the four elements. However, where dry land emerges from water, on the land, all four elements interact, making living creatures possible. This concept continued until the seventeenth century CE (Christian era) when Copernicus proposed that the sun, not the earth, was the center of the universe. As time passed and technology improved, Galileo, Newton, Hubbell, and a host of others allowed us to realize that not only was the earth not the center of the universe, but it was part of an extremely vast and probably continuously expanding universe.

Accompanying this sketch of the philosophical and astronomical aspects of belief in the earth as the center of the universe are a number of other events and actors that help in our consideration of this topic.

Aristotle's view was that the four elements existed in concentric circles. Muslim, Hebrew, and Christian philosophers saw in the abnormality in perfect concentric circles when dry land emerges from water an opportunity to emphasize a creator god as the reason for this abnormality. Most philosophers found that answer unsatisfactory and gave major alternate reasons why the abnormality developed. The last of these reasons was that there are no separate spheres of earth and water. This view was not widely accepted immediately; however, with the discovery of a new continent by Columbus, that view was accepted as a reality. The events and activities in this section are consistent with the summary of events and activities in the previous section.

Medical Concepts and Treatments

It should be obvious by now that my experience tells me that our perception of the world and the events in it is determined by each person's personal experiences as modulated by the cultural and social influences present in those personal experiences. The phenomenon described in this section should help to enforce that position.

The concept I am recommending I call *biological humanism.* Most of us, at some time in our educational pursuit, took a course titled biology. The term *biology*[8] was first introduced by Linnaeus in 1736. However, Aristotle[9] (d. 322 BCE) wrote several books covering subjects that today would be considered biology—*Generation of Animals, Movement of Animals, Progression of Animals,* and *Parts of Animals.* So, thought about what we today call biology has a somewhat lengthy history. My premise in referring to *biological humanism* is that we are primarily *biological* beings and only secondarily *human* beings.

The substance of that premise, although not stated as I have stated it here, also has an extensive history in human thought. Currently, it is referred to as the mind-body problem.[10*] The mind-body problem is relevant here because it, along with other concepts we have previously considered, provides a framework for our being able to understand how some of the concepts being considered here were able to be maintained as viable in human society.

Bloodletting[11] *as Medical Treatment.* Bloodletting as a medical treatment arose from the concept of *humors*,[12] bodily fluids, that relate to the health state of the human body. While the concept of humors may have developed in ancient Egypt or Mesopotamia, thought about an imbalance of humors as a source of illness or disease was systematized by Hippocrates (d. 370 BCE) in ancient Greece. Humors were blood, phlegm, yellow bile, and black bile (black bile was considered the source of depression). If all of these substances existed in proper proportions, the body would be healthful; if they were out of proportion or balance, the body would become ill. Bloodletting was devised as a means of obtaining proper balance among the humors.

Galen (129–ca. 200 CE) was one of the most famous early professional physicians. His prolific work and writing and his popularity offered such significance to the concept of humors (and therefore bloodletting) that the concept prevailed for about 1,300 years. Galen promoted the idea that blood was the dominant humor and therefore the one that most needed to be controlled.

Galen had discovered the difference between venous and arterial blood, based on the difference in color. He developed a complex system of how much and what type (arterial or venous) should be removed based on the patient's age,

---

* In addition to the false dichotomy between mind and body mentioned earlier (Descartes's error), in ancient Greek philosophy, the mind-body problem led to the development of the concept of *soul*—a problematic concept in our attempt to abandon the idea of god.

state of health, the weather, and the location at which the bloodletting should occur. More serious diseases required more extensive bloodletting. Fevers required highly extensive bloodletting.

From our modern perspective, it seems obvious that bloodletting, especially excessive bloodletting as required in some situations by the then existing practices, would have weakened an already sick body to the point that recovery would have been hindered rather than helped. However, because the practice was fostered by a socially accepted and established authority, it continued over centuries.

Bloodletting was so fully accepted as a practice that it was not until the 1800s that the practice began to be questioned. Even in the early 1900s, medical practitioners in Boston who were not using bloodletting as a treatment for pneumonia were judged negligent.[13] Today, bloodletting is rarely, if ever, used. A highly respected and commonly used practice has now been abandoned in human society as more detrimental than useful.

Germs Are the Cause of All Disease—Or Are They? The idea that germs, specifically, cause disease was not formulated until the mid-1600s. Prior to that, from the late pre-Christian era, both in the East and the West, disease was thought to be caused by miasma[14]—bad air. Bad air was thought to be caused by invisible seeds in the air. Galen fostered this concept by describing various types of "bad air seeds" for various diseases. These bad air seeds were thought to be spontaneously generated by various substances. Maggots were also thought to be spontaneously generated. In an experiment conducted in about 1668, the experimenter, Reide, filled three jars with a meatloaf and an egg. He covered two of the jars, one tightly and one loosely, with gauze, and left the third jar open. In a few days, he noticed that the contents of the open jar were covered with maggots; a few maggots were found on the gauze of the loosely covered jar; no maggots were found on the tightly sealed jar. He noticed that flies had availed themselves to the open jars but not the sealed jar. He concluded that the maggots were generated by the flies, not spontaneously generated.

With the demise of the belief in spontaneous generation, and with the discovery of miniature bodies (germs) with the development of the microscope in the early 1700s, the contagion theory of disease as caused by germs became generally accepted. New health practices developed based on the germ concept of disease. In Italy, Bassi, in 1885, recommended boiling water to eliminate the germs to make it safe for drinking. Pasteur developed a process for making milk germ-free in the early 1860s.

On another front, the attempt to find a cure for scurvy was being pursued. Scurvy is described as a "hideous disease" that was particularly prominent among participants in extended sea voyages. Gratzer[15] recounts numerous situations in which seamen with rather severe cases of scurvy had the disease remitted or completely cured when ships would stop at locations where fresh fruit was available and consumed. However, no one made the connection that the absence in the diet of some substance present in the fruit was the cause of scurvy, although a book, *Discourse on the Scurvy,* was published that, with some sarcasm, reported accounts of sailors with extreme cases of scurvy having been cured by citrus juice. The author indicated that it was obvious that scurvy was "a kind of corruption of the blood" (think miasma). However, in 1747, James Lind conducted an experiment[*] aboard the *Salisbury.* When severe scurvy

* Gratzer suggests that this may have been the first controlled clinical trial.

broke out, he divided the affected seamen into six groups. All were fed the same basic diet. However, each group received a different kind of supplement that was considered potentially beneficial. The supplement for one group consisted of two oranges and one lemon per day. After six days, the men who had received the supplement of oranges and a lemon were free of the symptoms of scurvy, ready for duty, and assigned as nurses for the others in the test.

The experiment described above was a major step in the discovery that sometimes disease is caused by the *absence* of something in the diet as opposed to the *introduction* to the body of something from the outside.

Subsequent experiments such as the one above, along with the invention of improved methods of examination of more minuscule components and activities of the human body (i.e., electron microscope), allowed the discovery of many dietary requirements not previously known. The discovery of those dietary requirements led to the development of nutritional supplements—vitamins and minerals, particularly trace minerals, which could be taken orally or intravenously.

Abandonment of the idea that germs are the cause of all diseases and acceptance of the idea that some diseases are caused by the absence of substances in the diet provided the opportunity for a more healthful life, thereby benefiting human existence.

Radical Mastectomy Is a Cure for Breast Cancer.[16] To have become a cancer survivor is to have beaten cancer at its own game—cancer is a survivor par excellence. Cancer has been described as "a parallel species, one perhaps more adapted to survival than even we are,"[17]—an apt description since more people die of cancer than are cured of it.

The original name for this disease, *karkinos,* for the Greek word for "crab," was suggested by Hippocrates about

400 BCE. Not unexpectedly, early treatment for cancer focused on a series of bleeding and purging rituals to accommodate the emphasis on humors (described above), promoted specifically by Galen. However, by the fifteenth century, some surgeons were attempting to excise cancerous lesions. Some of the most influential surgeons of the time, however, advised against surgical procedures in the treatment of cancer.

When the concept of humors was essentially abandoned, a number of relatively closely occurring circumstances allowed surgery to become the preferred method of treatment of cancer. In 1808, Matthew Baillie published *The Morbid Anatomy of Some of the Most Important Parts of the Human Body,* based largely on the work of an uncle who had performed extensive, experimental surgical removal of cancer on animals and cadavers. This publication provided a foundation for surgical removal of tumors. Additionally, in 1846, anesthesia was first demonstrated and rapidly became an accepted practice. In 1865–1867, Joseph Lister demonstrated that a carbolic acid paste could be used as an antiseptic to assist in the healing of surgical wounds. Armed with these three new tools, surgeons were set to establish surgical removal as the recommended "cure" for all types of cancer.

William Stewart Hallstead was the physician most prominently associated with the concept of radical mastectomy,* not because he invented the procedure but because of his prominence as a surgeon and his sincere dedication to the belief that radical mastectomy was the only cure for breast cancer.

When Hallstead became a surgical intern in the

* Willie Meyer invented the radical mastectomy contemporaneously with Hallstead but never acquired the public affiliation with the procedure that Hallstead did.[18]

mid-1870s, the practices just described were well established surgical processes. Initially, only the immediately affected areas were excised. However, when operated patients' cancer began to recur, one of Hallstead's students began to keep a visual record of the areas of recurrence and noticed that the cancer seemed to recur at the margins of the previous surgery. Also, recurrence would frequently exist in nearby lymph nodes. Based on this information, the area of excision began to be expanded. Soon that expansion moved to areas of the neck and shoulder. Mastectomy had indeed become radical.

However, the procedure was hardly a cure. In 1907, in a presentation Hallstead made to the American Surgical Association, he divided his patients based on whether before surgery the cancer had spread to nearby lymph nodes. Of the sixty patients with no cancer-afflicted nodes, forty-five had been cured of breast cancer at five years. Of the forty patients *with* affected nodes, only three had survived. It was evident that how extensive the surgery was did not determine the survival rate; survival depended on how extensively the cancer had spread before surgery.

These findings alone, however, were not the major cause of the demise of radical mastectomy. The discovery of alternate treatments for cancer, such as x-ray and chemotherapy, eventually led to the abandonment of radical mastectomy as the cure for breast cancer.

The pattern for establishment and abandonment of ideas holds here. An idea is developed, supported by a societally accepted authority, continues for a significant period of time, often to the detriment of at least some members of human society, and is only reluctantly abandoned when a viable alternative to the practice occurs.

Hail, the Mighty Magnet[19] *(But Don't Get It Near Garlic!)*[20]

Why introduce this topic, especially the garlic issue? First, consider why the magnet was mighty.

Magnets[21] (frequently called "loadstones") were described by the sixth century BCE in Greece and the fourth century BCE in China. Findings by archaeologists suggest that by these times, or possibly even earlier, humans were using magnets to orient the placement of buildings to the north. Magnets soon became useful in compasses for orienting ships. Columbus's and Magellan's voyages were made possible partially because of compasses.

By the early 1700s, England was prominently developing their seafaring activities. Compasses were a prominent part of this expansion. Ships had several different kinds of compasses located in various places on the ships. The increasing seafaring activities produced increased business and financial benefits for British society. The general population benefited from these increases and began to expand their appreciation for compasses and, therefore, for magnets in general.

Even before this practical application of magnets, magnets had been credited with highly diverse claims for their power. Before gravity was described, magnetism was considered the cause of many physical phenomena. The tides were considered caused by magnetism. Magnetism was considered to cause fermentation and the control of the sun over plants. Some sorts of vegetables, though set at a distance, were thought to attract each other by magnetism. Snakes were thought to attract prey to themselves by magnetism. Almost any incident of attraction was considered to be the result of magnetism.

Magnets were also thought to have a large range of

practical uses. Magnets were used by medical personnel to attempt to draw foreign substances from the body. Magnets were considered particularly useful for treating tooth ache, gout, and rheumatism. Specific types of magnets were developed for various situational uses. Magnetism was considered the cause of conception; magnets were used in delivery and in attempting to prevent miscarriages. Magnets were even used to detect adultery.

From another perspective, arguments about magnetism were used to defend the biblical stories of the flood, Armageddon, and numerous other biblical phenomena. Magnets and magnetism were a pervasive and seemingly consuming passion of the general public. "Hail, the mighty magnet."

Second, what about the prohibition of associating magnets and garlic? The substance of the prohibition was that garlic caused magnets to be ineffective. To most (if not all) of us, that seems obviously and blatantly wrong. I introduce it exactly for that reason. To us, it seems blatantly wrong for at least two reasons. First, we have grown accustomed to experimentation as an expected cultural phenomenon. And second, as I suggested in the previous chapter, we are in many ways uninformed. Before I read Wootton's discussion of this topic, I was unaware that society generally had, for an extended period of time, held this belief.

I could find no references indicating when the concept developed that garlic would disable a magnet. Wootton's discussion of the property of magnets was set in the context of describing the importance of facts and experiments in the development of science. He was describing the difficulty of interpreting the writings of della Porta, whose books were published in the mid-1500s. della Porta was familiar with the writings of Garzoni, who evidently had stated that there is much nonsense written about magnets and that reliable knowledge has to be based on experience. Garzoni had suggested that with a couple of magnets and some iron bars, one could discover that there was no anonymity between magnets and garlic. Della Porta evidently tried the experiment and discovered that even when a magnet was bathed in garlic juice, it did not lose its power of attraction. Evidently, the premise also existed that if a magnet had lost its power, the power could be restored by washing the magnet in goat's blood. della Porta tried that process and discovered that it also was false.

Evidently, since magnets had the unusual capacity to attract other solid substances, and because magnets had gained social acceptance because of their usefulness in navigation, folklore about their capacities and the undoing of those capacities had been confabulated by a society that was unaccustomed to experimentation or testing to determine the validity of their beliefs. It was only when science began to develop, based on experimentation, that society was able and willing to abandon their confabulated system of beliefs about magnets.

An Eyewitness Is the Best Proof of the Validity of a Circumstance

Eyewitnesses have been used as the primary source in determining the validity of circumstances in legal situations at least as long as recorded history. The Code of Ur-Nammu[22] contains two items related to the responsibility of eyewitnesses in legal situations. That practice was based on the premise that if one sees something, what one sees must be true, and therefore, one would be able to report accurately the circumstances of what one had seen. That premise seemed so obvious that for thousands of years we humans have depended on it.

While the subject of whether what one sees is real has long been a question of philosophical debate, with the invention of neuroscience and the investigation of memory, one's ability to remember accurately what one has seen has come into question, and along with it, sincere questioning of the absolute accuracy of eyewitness testimony. Michael Gazzaniga[23*] gives several examples from actual legal cases in which eyewitness testimony that appeared to be unquestionable turned out to be totally wrong.

In one case, a woman who had been raped in her home gave very specific details about the face of the rapist. A suspect was identified, and the woman was absolutely sure she had identified the proper person. However, the person identified was being interviewed on TV at the exact time the rape occurred. Police later realized that the victim had been watching that TV interview when she was attacked, and the victim had misattributed the face of the person she had seen in the interview as the rapist.

Numerous other instances exist of misattribution or misinformation based on false memories by eyewitnesses. Accordingly, with the development of newer technologies for identifying the presence of suspects at crime scenes, such as DNA analysis, eyewitness testimony, while still used, is not considered the primary source of reliable information about the circumstances in legal situations. Likely, at some point, eyewitness testimony will be abandoned as a determinant in legal situations.

* While the reasons for the memory distortions described are not directly germane to our consideration here, understanding those reasons is important in our understanding of who we are as humans. This source is worth your consideration on many levels.

Summary

In some fashion, each of the ideas discussed in this chapter originated from human perception. When the perceptions were questioned and questioning was supported by substantial evidence, which gained adequate social acceptance, the ideas were usually abandoned, to the benefit of human society as a whole.

Abandoning the Idea of God

> The evolutionary future of religion is extinction.
> —Wallace[24]

The existence of the idea of god in human society follows the same pattern as the other ideas discussed in this chapter. The idea of god was confabulated based on human perceptions. Although the actual existence of god has occasionally been questioned (more about that in the next chapter), no systematic treatment of the nonexistence of god has ever gained wide social acceptance. Accordingly, the idea of god, and belief in the actual existence of god, is extensively accepted.

When Matthews wrote about the idea of god in 1931, he did not directly recommend abandoning the idea of god. He did, however, place belief in god in a larger context of religion generally, thus laying a foundation upon which abandoning the idea of god can be built. Wallace, in 1966, constructed the framework that required serious consideration of abandoning the idea of god. Also in 1966, Berger and Luckmann, with the introduction of the concept of social constructionism, provided the application of "siding" effects, which would make abandoning the idea of god livable. With the establishment of the society for neuroscience 1969 and forward, and the advances in understanding of numerous aspects of human existence, highlighted by intricate understanding of neural activity that produces feelings, thoughts, and consciousness, the furnishings required for serious consideration of the abandonment of the idea of god are in place.

Additionally, advances in understanding the universe in which we humans live lend peripheral support to abandoning the idea of god. With the original development of the telescope, we were able to abandon, eventually, (in spite of strenuous, adamant objection by religious authorities) the idea that the earth is the center of the universe. Since the structure for abandoning the idea of god was built, we have developed telescopes that allow us to interpret activities that led to the existence of our universe, our planet, and ourselves. We can see almost unlimited distances, both in time and space. No discoveries have been made that support the cosmic view required for belief in the creator/sustainer god that is presented in traditional theistic religious belief. The extinction of the idea of god is a sleeping beauty idea whose time for awakening has arrived.

However, on a personal level, I am aware of the difficulty of abandoning the idea of god. One does not easily abandon an idea that has seemingly been useful, and even helpful, without something equally or more potentially useful and helpful. That something is our next matter of consideration.

Chapter 5

When Humans Abandon the Idea of God, What's Next?

Throughout history people have discarded a conception of God when it no longer works for them.[1]

Belief in supernatural powers is doomed to die out, all over the world, as a result of the increasing adequacy and diffusion of scientific knowledge and of the realization by secular forces that supernatural belief is not necessary.[2]

We can never forget enough of our familiar present to reconstruct in our minds any past in its full integrity.[3]

Background—General

Nontheistic thought is neither a new nor an only recent phenomenon in humans. Humans have existed for at least two hundred thousand years. Humans did not confabulate the idea of god until about fifty thousand years ago. That humans did not *think* prior to fifty thousand years ago is inconceivable. All thinking done by humans prior to their having confabulated the idea of god would have been nontheistic thought. Similarly, as the brain is a recent development in our life as biological beings, theistic thought is a recent development in humans.

How did ancient humans transmit information among themselves? They invented language.[4] How and when language was invented remains a highly debated question, more so about the how than the when. A prominently considered view is that language was invented between one hundred thousand and sixty thousand years ago. On that premise, the idea of god was confabulated within 10–40,000 years after language was invented. With the invention of language, civilization became possible.[5] Civilization began among humans in a nontheistic environment.

Humans invented writing about fifty thousand years ago. How did humans, during the forty-five thousand years from the time they confabulated the idea of god until they invented writing, sustain and disseminate the idea of god? According to Marshall McLuhan, "until writing was invented, man lived in acoustic space."[6] Study of how information was disseminated before writing was invented is called *orality*.[7]

Orality, as it is currently used, is thought and verbal expression in cultures in which modern technologies, including writing and printing, are nonexistent (primary orality) as opposed to cultures in which thought and verbal expression *do* depend on writing and other technological media (secondary orality). Obviously, for our consideration here, primary orality is our concern.

How and when did orality develop as an area of academic study? The *Iliad* and the *Odyssey* (probably composed in late eighth or seventh century BCE) were the focal point in its development. For more than two thousand years, scholars have studied these two works of Homer, usually under the presumption that they had originally been composed in writing. While during this time, the poetry was highly respected, if not revered, occasionally some examiners had questions about the nature of the authorship of the poetry. During the 1600s, one Italian philosopher of history suggested that the poetry was somehow the creation of a whole people and not of a single author.

In the early 1700s, an English archaeologist who had carefully identified some of the places referred to in those works concluded that it was Homer's power of memory that had enabled him to produce the poetry. He further suggested that memory played a considerably different role in oral cultures than in cultures in which formal writing occurred.

In the early nineteenth century, a group of scholars, called the Analysts, described the texts of Homer's work as combinations of earlier poems or fragments and attempted to determine how the bits had been assembled. While not fully successful in their endeavor, their suggestion eventually enabled others to begin to see Homer's works somewhat differently. In the early 1900s, Milman Parry, in his doctoral dissertation, demonstrated that "virtually every distinctive feature of Homeric poetry is due to the economy enforced on it by oral methods of composition."[8] Further study of this premise revealed that the poet had used different terms for *wine* and that each was metrically different. As an oral poet, Homcr used his varied terms for wine to fit the meter of the lines as he orally recited the poem—differently at each recital.

Additional verification of this concept was accomplished by Albert Lord in the mid-1900s. In the country then called Yugoslavia, Parry had discovered contemporary oral poets who composed epic narratives for which there were no written texts. Lord[9] continued Parry's work and built a very large collection of oral recordings of modern Yugoslav narrative poets. Interviews with the poets about the recordings revealed that the poets believed they had repeated songs in exactly the same way each time they had recited them. However, replaying the recordings revealed that while the rhythm and meter of the songs were exactly the same, the words frequently differed. Further, it was discovered that a poet who was learning a new song preferred to wait a day or so before repeating it, apparently to allow time for the story to settle into his own store of themes and formulas before repeating the song. Apparently, for the poet, the song consists of themes and formulas that are constructed into the song as it is sung, rather than being a memorization of the exact words and phrases of the song. This approach is the substance of primary orality in a society, or a portion of a society, that does not depend primarily on modern technologies. These concepts of primary orality can help us understand how ancient humans disseminated and sustained their confabulated idea of god.

Background—Phenomena Associated with Development of Humanism

Sensation (1)	Authority (2)	Nontheistic Thought (2)	Humanism (2)	Theism (3)	Atheism (4)
Origin of first cell, 4400 MYA	Origin of communal life, least 300,000 YA	All thought prior to 50,000 YA	Origin of communal life, at least 300,000 YA	50,000 YA	1580-90 CE
(Time Order Sequence)					

Figure 1

A number of phenomena have been associated with the development of humanism. Figure 1 names those phenomena and presents an approximate time when each of the phenomena began. The time of origin for each of the phenomena is indicated by the number in parentheses below the label for each of the phenomena. In the following discussion, each of the phenomena will be described and its relationship to the concept of humanism considered.

Probably, most people think of humanism as a recent development in human thought. That idea would be correct for the development of modern humanism; however, as figure 1 indicates, humanism has existed for at least three hundred thousand years—as early as humans began living together in any kind of organized group. Phenomena contributing to the development of the concept of humanism, however, are as old as life itself.

Human thought is obviously a result of humans being alive. Life, as previously suggested, is an entangled, complex, nonlinear phenomenon. Consideration of the relationships among theistic thought, nontheistic thought, humanism, and atheism demonstrates perfectly the complex, entangled, nonlinear nature of human thought. Reductionism, which began its heyday with the invention of science, obviously has made great contributions to human welfare. However, the relationships among nontheistic thought, theistic thought, humanism, and atheism are so entangled that a reductionist approach to their consideration is neither useful nor possible, as will be demonstrated in the following discussion.

Give yourself a moment to consider what each of these terms means. You probably have already done this, but if you haven't, consider also how you feel about each of the concepts. How extensive do you consider nontheistic thought to be today? Do you equate nontheistic thought and atheism? How extensively do you think humanism is considered as a preferred philosophy of life? Do you think humanism is atheism?

At the risk of being pedantic (and possibly even boring, at least to some of you), but to be as clear as possible in the following presentation, I will start with dictionary definitions[10] of the major terms currently being examined.

Sensation: "the operation or function of the senses, perception or awareness of stimuli through the senses; a mental condition or physical *feeling* resulting from stimulation of a sense organ ... ; A general *feeling* not directly attributable to any given stimulus ... A mental *feeling*, especially a state of excited *feeling* [emphasis added] ..."

Authority: "the power to determine, adjudicate, or otherwise settle issues or disputes; jurisdiction; the right to control, command, or determine; a power or right delegated or given; a person or body of persons in whom authority is vested ..."

Theistic: adjectival form of "theism"; "the belief in one god as the creator and ruler of the universe, without rejection of revelation (distinguished from deism); belief in the existence of a god or gods (opposed to atheism)"; origin: first recorded in 1670–80.

Humanism: "any system or mode of thought or action in which human interests, values, and dignity predominate; devotion to or study of the humanities"; origin: first recorded 1805–15.

Atheism: "the doctrine or belief that there is no god; disbelief in the existence of a supreme being or beings"; origin: 1580–90.

I'm about to ask you to do something that, according to the third epigram at the beginning of the chapter, is impossible. While we may not be able to reconstruct the past history and use of the concepts in the definitions just given, in full integrity, we need to try to sort out, as best as humanly possible, what these terms meant and how they are interrelated. The dates given in the preceding definitions refer to the time periods in which these words first appeared in the English language. The word *atheism* appeared in English before the word *theism*. The word *humanism* first appeared in English only about two hundred years ago. In the following discussion, obviously, we will be considering concepts that existed and were written about centuries before the English language was invented. Since many of us think, read, and write only in English, we may begin to understand the difficulty of reconstructing in its full integrity the thought processes involved in developing and disseminating these concepts.

Sensation. Eventually, for many of you (if you're still with us), the place you will attempt to hang your hat in defense of belief in the actual existence of god will be feelings. The subject of feelings, contrary to what you may think, is very complex and is therefore a subject to which we will return frequently as we proceed. Notice in the definition of *sensation* above the frequency with which the word *feeling* occurs. Culturally, we tend to equate feeling with the sense of touch. For example, if someone says something kind about us, we may respond, "I'm touched," meaning something like, "I feel good about what you said." The cause of that association is not accidental; the sense of touch is the oldest sense: "touch is the first sense prior to the differentiation into other sensory modalities."[11] Paterson, in chapter 4, claims an attempt to recover the hidden histories of touch. While his discussion of the history of touch is very thorough, he does not consider the prehistory of touch. As I have suggested previously, if we really want to understand who we are as humans, we must consider a much longer view of ourselves than history can show us.

As presented in figure 1, sensation/touch has been present since the origin of the first cell that led eventually to the development of our being human. As far as we are aware, cells operate today in the same fashion they originally developed. Several components communicate with one another through a process called signal transduction,[12] in which chemical or physical signals are transmitted through a cell as a series of molecular events. A chain of these events is known as a signaling pathway. Signaling pathways interact to form networks that allow cellular responses to be coordinated. Complexes of these pathways are called mechanotransduction pathways. Specialized forms of mechanotransduction pathways are responsible for mechanosensation, including touch. A sense of touch is one of the factors that allow us to have feelings. The basic mechanism for feelings is as old as cellular life itself. The interpretation, or meaning, of a specific feeling is, however, determined by the existing cultural milieu at the time the feeling occurs. The substrate for the feeling is ancient;[13] the meaning of the feeling is modern and culturally determined.

Authority. The definition of authority stated above obviously represents a modern cultural view of the term, which is almost diametrically opposite the original meaning and intent of the word. What was the original intent and meaning of the word *authority*? Hannah Arendt[14] reiterates the sense indicated in the third epigram at the beginning of this chapter, that our current view of the word *authority* almost entirely prevents our being able to understand what the original meaning of the word was. After an extended discussion of what authority originally meant, she concludes by saying,

"Authority precludes the use of external means of coercion; where force is used, authority has failed."[15]

What, then, was the original meaning of authority? The word *authority* originated in Roman culture.[16] Accordingly, it originated in a culture in which theism, extensive governmental organization, and writing existed. Because of those influences, it has long been held that they, particularly theism,[17] were the source of the concept of authority. The concept, however, originated in prior, primitive cultures in which none of those factors was present. Studies by anthropologists in primitive societies suggest other sources for the concept of authority.

E. Adamson Hoebel, in *The Law of Primitive Man: A Study in Comparative Legal Dynamics*,[18] describes his relationship with a Cheyenne interpreter, High Forehead, who previously worked as an interpreter for an anthropologist among the Cheyenne. The interpreter commented to Hoebel that the prior anthropologist never asked questions like the ones he was asking. As a result of the questions that Hoebel was asking, the interpreter came to realize that "the Cheyennes, his people, had, on their own responsibility in their time dealt with and met many problems of social order." One day, while they were resting, the interpreter said, *"The Indian on the Prairie, before there was the white man to put him in the guardhouse, had to have something to keep him from doing wrong* [emphasis added]."[19] That something was a sense of authority.

Hoebel, in another source,[20] suggests that the exercise of authority is a necessary component of group/social life and was present among our primate ancestors who preceded us. Further, he says that the most common form of authority in primitive societies is "internally created and accepted as right and good by those who are subject to its control."[21] Stated somewhat differently, "the complicity of the wills of all [people] is essential to establishing rightful public authority."[22] In primitive societies, authority existed in mutual agreement among members of the society as to what constituted acceptable behavior. (As we shall discover later, that concept is a basic premise of humanism.)

Implicit in this conception of authority is an assumption of "reasoned elaboration."[23] In an extended example of reasoned elaboration, Friedrich presents a discourse about how a child is carefully taught. In the beginning, a child is fully dependent on the power of the parents. Wise, thoughtful parents explain carefully to their children why certain behaviors are important and necessary. In this way, they develop in the child an understanding of and a participation in the reasons why parents ask for and expect obedience. That understanding in a family setting extends to other social settings in which the child participates and thereby understands and makes his or her own the behaviors and concepts that become a pattern of acceptable behavior. Thus, "discipline is transformed into self-discipline." In this context, authority becomes the ability "to enlarge upon what is being communicated in terms meaningful to those who are being addressed."[24]

How did we get from "where force is used, authority has failed," to "the right to control, command, or determine" as the meaning of authority? Theism and its subsequent influence on society in general appear, to me, to be the answer. While we haven't yet considered theism extensively, obviously theism places a great emphasis on authority as a right to control, command, or determine. According to Hendel,[25] the following statement represents the prevailing philosophical attitude from the time of Rome's dominance until recent time:

> Authority [was] a great universal fact of creation, with God's will the ultimate originative

> native power, and the freedom of created man is ultimately in accord, with the lawful, authoritative order of the state, so long as both reverently stand under the judgment of God.

While Hendel claims this position is no longer dominant in philosophy, it certainly dominates most current theistic thought, and theistic thought is highly predominant currently in society—therefore justifying the current dictionary definition of authority. The role of our concept of authority as humans is an important component in our consideration of what's next when humans abandon the idea of god.

Nontheistic thought. All thought that occurred before confabulation of the idea of god; thought by all biological beings who do not believe in the existence of supernatural beings.

Beginning Nontheistic Thought Humans Theism
[____________________________________X_____________.]

The graphic above shows the approximate relative time relationship between nontheistic thought, the origin of humans, and the origin of theistic thought. The line represents the timeframe for nontheistic thought; the . represents the timeframe for the existence of theistic thought.

What evidence exists that thought existed before the presence of humans? What might be considered evidence that thought exists? Planning is a pervasive activity among humans. What is planning? "Planning is the process of *thinking* (emphasis added) about the activities required to achieve a desired goal."[26] What are the basic steps in the process of planning? One must recognize a situation about which something needs to be done, propose a solution for the problem presented by the situation, and implement the solution. Performing those steps requires thinking, as indicated in the definition previously given.

Using tools requires a similar set of cognitive steps: one must recognize a situation in which a device would be useful in performing a task, find or invent a tool suitable for the task, and successfully use the tool to accomplish the task. Performing those tasks requires thinking. If nonhuman animals could be demonstrated as having the capacity to plan and/or use tools, that should be evidence of thinking.

Accounts are numerous of chimpanzees,[27] both in the wild and in laboratory situations, using tools. Several species of birds, but particularly Corvidae (crows, jays, and magpies), have been observed using tools. Recently, crows were, for the first time, witnessed *building* tools from various parts.[28] A crow had been trained to use a small rod to cause a parcel of food to be made available to it. The crow was then presented with a situation in which the rod had been shortened so that it was not long enough to perform the task. However, several rods that could be fitted together were present. After an unsuccessful attempt to retrieve the food, the crow placed two of the rods together, pressed the length against a solid surface to assure its stability, and successfully used the extended rod to cause the food particle to be available to it. That extended set of circumstances required thinking.

I personally became aware of animals' capacity for planning by observing an activity by one of my wire fox terriers, Abbey. I had a bird bath in my backyard, which Abbey occupied when outside. Birds would frequently flock around the birdbath, and when Abbey saw them, she would rush the birdbath, attempting to catch a bird. After a period of time of having repeated that activity, I saw her seated with her back to the pedestal of the birdbath, underneath the rim of the bowl of the birdbath. She waited until birds perched on the edge of the birdbath and then jumped out to try to catch one. Although she did not catch a bird, she had thought of a way to make the possibility of catching one more likely. That activity required the steps of planning: recognize a situation, propose a solution, put the solution into practice. Abbey was thinking.

Temple Grandin, an animal scientist with an acknowledged reputation in animal behavior, particularly animal emotions, also describes numerous situations[29] consistent with the concept of animal thought being considered here. Researchers set up a situation where a blue jay was required to hide mealworms in the tray of sand while other jays watched. When the experimenters took the watcher jays away, the hider jays immediately dug up the mealworms and re-hid them in other parts of the tray. In another example, researchers were testing two crows to determine whether they would choose a hooked wire or a straight wire for getting food out of a tube. In one session, one crow snatched the hooked wire away from the other, leaving the second crow with only the straight wire to use. When the crow with the straight wire realized it wouldn't work, she bent it into a hook. After using the hooked wire, she improved the wire by changing the angle until it was just the correct angle for retrieving the food.

Grandin reports one example of an experiment in which rats and humans had to look at a TV screen and press a lever within a time limit when a dot appeared in the top half of the screen. Since there was no punishment for a wrong response, the smartest strategy was to press the lever as often as the screen appeared. That's what the rats did. They just kept pressing the lever each time the screen changed. But the humans never figured this out. They kept trying to come up with a rule so sometimes they would press the bar and sometimes they wouldn't. The rats ended up with a lot more rewards than the humans.

In the prologue to his book *Wild Minds,* Mark Hauser[30] asks and answers (more extensively than I indicate here) a number of questions: "do animals have emotions; do animals communicate; are animals guided by instinct; do animals have rules by which they abide, and sometimes break?" His answer to each of these questions is yes. However, to the question, "Do animals think?" his answer is, "I think ... [this is an] unhelpful question." However, further in the book, he gives numerous illustrations of various animals' ability to understand the use of various devices as tools. He describes a chimpanzee named Sarah as "understanding that some objects are designed with specific functional roles, transforming other objects into alternative states."[31] He also claims that many animals understand that for a tool to be useful, it must have certain design characteristics. To me, it appears that all of these activities, which he mentions, require thinking.

Despite Hauser's reticence (we'll consider the reasons for his reticence later) in answering in the affirmative that animals think, certainly sufficient evidence exists to show that animals do think. It seems to me unlikely, however, that animals are theists-- that they believe in a supernatural god. On that premise, all thought by animals other than humans is nontheistic thought. Nontheistic thought has existed at least as long as animals have existed.

Humanism. While the word *humanism* first appeared in English in the early 1800s, the phenomenon of humanism as "a mode of thought or action in which human interests and values predominate" existed far into prehistory. Recall that in primitive societies, authority existed in mutual agreement among members of the society as to what constituted acceptable behavior. Authority was inherent because it produced behavior consistent with general human interests and values. Those patterns of behavior became the basis for what would eventually be called humanism. Therefore, humanism as a phenomenon of human life has existed since communal living among humans began, at least three hundred thousand years ago. Accordingly, it existed as an operational premise among humans when they confabulated the idea of god.

Since the core premise of humanism is mutual concern among humans for the welfare of one another, possibly the earliest written evidence of humanistic concerns is the code of Ur-Nammu[32] (2100–2050 BCE). The code is a list of legal responsibilities that provide for the welfare of citizens. The code is nontheistic. It makes no reference to theistic requirements in fulfilling the conditions of the code. It exists solely to promote the general well-being of the citizens of the society for which it was written.

It seems highly unlikely that this code of behavior originated with and was developed solely by King Ur-Nammu. Knowing that before writing was invented, all cultural phenomena were transmitted orally, it seems reasonable that Ur-Nammu assembled the items of his written code from an existing oral code. Thinking back even further, it seems highly likely that humanistic codes of behavior existed and were transmitted orally by primitive humans even before they confabulated the idea of god. Humanistic thought is likely older than theistic thought.

As suggested earlier, theism played a major role in changing the understanding of the meaning of authority, thereby relegating the existing phenomenon of humanism to a less important position in human affairs. By the time Roman culture developed, humanism was seen as nontheistic.

What was the nature of humanism in Roman culture? Remember that since humanism was not formalized as a concept until the early 1800s, none of the people discussed in ancient cultures were considered humanist. They are considered here because their thought processes embraced many of the concepts currently considered humanistic. Thinking about life and its meaning was subsumed under the heading of philosophy.

Possibly the earliest philosopher in Western culture to present ideas of a humanistic bent was Thales of Miletus[33] (c. 626–545 BCE). Thales is credited with departing from the use of mythology to explain the world and universe and instead using natural objects and phenomena as the basis for his philosophical explanations. He explained nature as deriving from a unity of everything based on the existence of a single ultimate substance. Accordingly, his explanation of the origins of the universe was nontheistic.

Xenophanes[34] (c. 570–475 BCE) was a Greek philosopher, theologian, poet, and social and religious critic. He is credited as the founder of a line of philosophy that culminated in Pyrrhonism. His writings are described as displaying skepticism, a view that became more prominent about a century later. I referred to Xenophanes in chapter 1 as possibly having been the first known person to have proposed the concept that humans created the idea of god.

Prodicus[35] (c. 465–395 BCE) was part of the first generation of Sophists who interpreted religion through the framework of naturalism; that is, he regarded the gods as personifications of the sun, moon, rivers, and anything else that provides comfort in human life. He believed that primitive humans were so impressed with what nature provided for the furtherance of life that they believed them to be provided by gods. Some evidence exists that Prodicus was charged with atheism. While his basic thought pattern was seemingly theistic, he did manifest some evidence of nontheistic-humanistic thought.

Democritus[36] (c. 460–370 BCE) is credited (possibly in conjunction with his mentor, Leucippus) with having invented the concept that all matter is composed of atoms. This concept would be exploited and expanded significantly by later philosophers whose intent was more clearly humanistic.

Pyrrhonism, named after Pyrrho[37] (c. 360–270 BCE), was a skeptical philosophical stance in which through suspension of judgment one is able to reach a condition of living well. Because our senses are unreliable, we should not depend on them—hence suspension of judgment. The process of making decisions described by the Pyrrhoists show signs of Buddhist philosophical influence, which Pyrro is said to have acquired during a stay in India. The significance of that connection will be considered later.

Marcus Tullius Cicero[38] (106–43 BCE) was a prolific philosopher and orator who is sometimes considered a humanist. One of his most famous works (BCE 45) is *The Nature of the Gods*.[39] The work is presented as a dialogue among three friends, although Cicero is not an active participant in the discussion, about the nature of the gods. Velleius first presents the Epicurean view of the gods, followed by a rebuttal from Cotta. Next, Balbus presents the Stoic view, which Cotta refutes. The work ends with a statement by Cicero that Vellius thought the arguments of Cotta were most true but that he thought the arguments of Balbus seemed to have the greater possibility.

Since, according to Cicero's concluding statement, he considers Balbus's arguments the most likely, he would be agreeing with the Stoics. The basic tenant of Stoicism[40] is that god and nature are the same. One's responsibility is to develop self-control and fortitude as a means of overcoming destructive emotions and thereby attaining a status of happiness. Therefore, while not directly denying the existence of god, Cicero's indication of acceptance of Stoicism probably is the source of his being considered a humanist.

Possibly the most obviously humanistic writer in ancient Greece was Titus Lucretius Carus[41] (c. 94–c. 55 BCE). His major work, *De rerum natura (On the Nature of Things)*, is a poem (in the Homeric tradition) of six untitled books, in didactic hexameter. While in his opening he mentions some of the gods in the traditional Roman pantheon, his overall tone throughout is critical of anything supernatural. He writes extensively about the evils of superstition, criticizes the concept of *creatio ex nihilo,* and repeatedly, and in detail, describes the concept of atoms, their properties, their movements, and the laws under which they operate.

The entirety of books 3 and 4 describe human life. In these descriptions, he makes frequent comparisons between the actions and behaviors of humans and other animals. He describes a unified life-mind-body concept and concludes that all components perish together; therefore, the fear of death is a folly as death merely extinguishes all feelings—both good and bad. Book 4 in its entirety discusses his theory of the senses: sight, hearing, taste, smell, and includes a discussion of sleep and dreams, love, and sex.

Book 5 might be considered a sweeping conclusion of what life might be like for humans who follow his philosophical thought. While this presentation may appear to have been highly speculative on his part and appear to us possibly unscientific, considering the time in which he wrote, it may be seen as highly intuitive and possibly even prophetic.

With this much emphasis on humanistic thought by various philosophers, why did humanism not gain greater acceptance? Possibly, the nature of life in the polis,[42] particularly religious life,[43] prevented the acceptance of humanism. Originally, the term *polis* referred to the administrative and religious city center as distinct from the rest of the city.

Eventually, however, it came to mean the entire body of citizens. Even with the change in meaning of the term, the original emphasis on civic and religious practices was retained. The chief focus of religion was on the correct practice of prayer, ritual, and sacrifice and was considered a source of social order. The Roman military followed a similar pattern. Military success depended on proper religious practices before and after battle. With this kind of structure, authority was vested in adherence to civic and religious traditions. Humanism, with its emphasis on mutual human responsibility to one another, was inconsistent with that structure and therefore not acceptable.

What was happening elsewhere during this basic time period? In many Eastern countries, several religious traditions were developing. In Japan, Shintoism,[44] a polytheistic religion, developed about 1000 BCE. In China, Confucius (551–479 BCE) considered himself a recodifier and retransmitter of a system of values inherited from about 1600 years BCE. Confucianism[45] is considered a system of thought and behavior with a particular emphasis on the importance of the family and social harmony, rather than on an otherworldly source of spiritual values. Also in China, in the fourth century BCE, Taoism[46] developed. A chief emphasis of Taoism is how to keep human behavior in accordance with the alternating cycles of nature.

In India, Hinduism[47] developed about 500 BCE. Hinduism is a diverse tradition spanning monotheism, polytheism, pantheism, monism, and possibly even atheism. Buddhism, a nontheistic religion and philosophy, also developed about 500 BCE.

Judaism[48] evolved from ancient Israelite religions about 500 BCE. A unique feature of Judaism was its monotheistic emphasis.

In numerous other scattered locations around the world,

small groups of people were developing their own concept of god. The religion of the Lingua, described in chapter 1, is an example of this type of religious development. Academically, the religion of this type of small group is called "indigenous religion."[49] The view of god or gods in indigenous religions (as in all religions) is determined by the cultural setting in which the view of god arises.

What does this review tell us about the development of humanism? At about the same time, in numerous locations and various cultural settings, many groups of humans were attempting to determine the best way to live meaningful lives in relationship with one another. To a large extent, the view of authority in the society was a major determinant in the view of god they adopted.

What about more recent humanism? The history of humanism appears (to me) to consist of six stages: a prehistorical stage which existed since communal living among humans began; an ancient stage, discussed above, culminating in the works of Cicero and Lucretius; a "patristic fathers" stage, beginning about the second century CE; a classic stage during the fourteenth through sixteenth century; a quiescent stage from the seventeenth to about the middle of the nineteenth century; and a modern stage from the middle of the nineteenth century to the present.

Giuseppe Toffanin's *History of Humanism*[50*] reaches back briefly into stage two, covers in exquisite detail stages three and four, and hints at what is to be expected in stage five. The following discussion is almost entirely dependent on my interpretation of his analysis. To provide a vantage point for the connection between stages one and two, he claims that for the first five centuries of the Christian era,

[*] Toffanin's *History* was first published in 1933 in Italy, was reprinted in 1940 and 1943, and was republished in 1950. The first American edition was published in 1954.

humanism and Christian thought stood side by side. He uses as an example to prove his point Victorinus (270–303 CE),[51] whom Augustine considered a rationalist. He also states, "The history of humanism will compel us continuously to revert to this starting point."[52] Accordingly, the history of humanism can be considered a duologue between theistic thought and rationalistic humanism.

This duologue during stage two was complicated by the influence of governmental authority and the increasing development of a church hierarchy. In 325 CE, Constantine I[53] convened the first Council of Nicaea,[54] which adopted the original Nicene Creed, fixed the date of Easter, settled a theological issue that was in dispute, and recognized various locations as authoritative representatives of the Christian Church. Between 325 and 787 CE, six more councils were held. By 449, at the second Council of Ephesus, the council began deposing individuals who did not strictly adhere to the doctrinal tenets proclaimed by the church. Many of the beliefs of those who were deposed would have been considered humanistic. Humanism, a concept that had existed since humans first began to live together in societal groups, became a sleeping beauty that would not rouse again until the fourteenth century.

And rouse again she did. Toffanin's consideration of the magnificence of the art, music, architecture, poetry, and so on is outstanding. He particularly emphasized the genius of Dante and the influence he has had on numerous other artists. Also, in addition to the magnificence of the areas mentioned, humanism was revived. The works of many writers from the ancient stage were revived and republished, particularly Cicero and Lucretius. Lucretius's *De rerum natura* was rediscovered in 1417 and had an extended influence on numerous writers during the Renaissance.[55]

However, the arts were not the only area that flourished.

Science was also invented, and scientific approaches came to depend on a new form of rationalism that overshadowed the rationalism of humanism. Humanism once again became a sleeping beauty.

Humanism began to rouse again in the early 1800s. Modern humanism[56] is a microcosm of the overall history of humanism. Public acceptance remains sporadic, and it continues as a duologue between nontheism and theism. In 1808,[57] a Bavarian educator coined the term *humanismus* to describe a planned curriculum in the classics. The term became widely accepted when it began to be used to describe the movement that flourished in the Italian Renaissance to revive classical learning. From that time, humanism attained the dual meaning of, on one hand, a philosophy of life and, on the other hand, a system of study about the classics.

After the French Revolution (1787–1799) and its sweeping social changes, humanistic ideas were strongly opposed by influential religious and political figures, and modern humanism began to be seen in a negative light, including being seen as atheistic, or at least secularistic.[58] Secularistic organizations support the philosophical view that moral standards should be based solely on concern for the good of humanity in the present—a view, as we have seen, that has existed since humans first began to live together in social groups. Wikipedia lists 104 secularist organizations in twenty-six countries, thirty-one of which are in the United States. All of these organizations might be considered humanistic organizations, although many are concerned primarily with what might be considered purely political issues, rather than social or moral issues.

In the United States, in 1927, an organization that began in Chicago, called the Humanist Fellowship,[59] began publishing the *New Humanist* magazine. In 1933 *A Humanist Manifesto*,[60] the first of three, was published. This manifesto referred to humanism as a religious movement to replace previous religions that were based on allegations of supernatural revelation. It contained fifteen points whose outlook described a worldwide society based on voluntary mutual cooperation. The *A* in the title was meant to indicate that the setting of humanistic ideals was an ongoing process and that the document did not represent dogma but would serve as a guide in developing a humanistic society. In 1941, the Humanist Fellowship became the American Humanist Association (AHA).

Humanist Manifesto II was written in 1973. It contained seventeen points, such as opposition to racism and weapons of mass destruction, maintained support for divorce and birth control, and the idea that technology can improve life. It proposed an international court, an item that has subsequently been implemented. The document was circulated and gained thousands of signatories.

Humanist Manifesto III was published in 2003. It contains seven primary themes, echoing much of the previous manifestos but with a higher focus on direct human responsibility and activity in maintaining a mutually interdependent human society. Signatories included twenty-one Nobel laureates.

Since 1953, the AHA has selected a humanist of the year. The list[61] includes the names of people from various walks of life who have contributed significantly to the overall welfare of human life.

Despite this extended history, humanism has never become a predominant phenomenon overall in human society. One area that differs slightly in this context is medicine. Hippocrates (460–370 BCE) was a Greek physician to whose name the Hippocratic oath[62] for physicians is attached. Current scholarship about the oath suggests that Hippocrates may not have been the original author, although it may have been written in the fourth or fifth century BCE. Modern translations into Greek of the oath, based on reconstructions from ancient fragments and full translations from the Vatican library of the tenth to eleventh century CE, record the oath as beginning, "I swear by Apollo physician, by, Asclepius, by Hygieia, by Panacea, and by all the gods and goddesses, etc. ..." By the twelfth century CE, the reference to the pantheon of gods had been deleted, and the text was presented in the form of a cross, showing the influence of Christianity. In 1847, the American Medical Association, and at about the same time the British general medical councils, issued revised versions of a medical oath. These revised documents provided a comprehensive overview of the obligations and professional behavior of a doctor to their patients and wider society, reflecting a humanistic bent. In 1948, the World Medical Association issued a much revised oath for physicians called the Declaration of Geneva. It began, "I swear to fulfill, to the best of my ability and judgment, this covenant: ..." Recent surveys of medical schools in the United States show that most use the revised versions. The influence of humanistic principles appears to have prevailed in the medical profession's expectations of its practitioners. In spite of this progression in the medical field, elsewhere in society, humanism remains a sleeping beauty. We shall return to this issue later.

Theism. If you are a believer, you probably thought, before you began reading this book (and possibly still do), that humans have always believed in god. However, as illustrated in the timeline earlier in this chapter, theistic thought is a mere (.) in the overall time frame of life. Also, if you are a believer, you possibly think that all theistic thought is monotheistic. The approximate population of the world is 15.6 billion.[63] An estimated 7.3 billion people are associated with a theistic religion; approximately 4.5 billion are affiliated with a monotheistic religion.[64] Theistic thought, particularly monotheistic thought, is a minority phenomenon among humans.*

Theistic thought comes in at least six flavors: monotheism, polytheism, pantheism, deism, autotheism, and value-judgment theism.[65] Of the 4.5 billion people who are affiliated with a monotheistic religion, approximately 2.3 billion, or about one-seventh, are Christians.

Polytheism is most often expressed in the form of belief in a pantheon of gods, with each having a specific role associated with a specific portion of the human life. The gods of the ancient Greeks and Romans were pantheistic. The extent that pantheism exists today would most likely be in societies where folk religions still exist. About half a million people are currently associated with folk religions. Pantheism[66] is usually considered a more philosophical than religious thought process. Pantheists essentially believe that everything is divine; no personal association exists between humans and the divine: everything is divine. Pantheists would likely be listed among the approximately one billion people identified as religious but unaffiliated with a specific religious tradition.

Deism[67] is also a largely philosophical stance. The major premise of deism is that knowledge of the world is not revealed but a product of human thought. Similarly to pantheists, deists would likely be listed among the approximately one billion people listed as unaffiliated.

Autotheism claims that divinity is inherently within oneself. Some elements of Hinduism and Buddhism claim

* While I am not aware of any enumeration of humanists in the world, one might suggest (possibly stretching a bit) that humanistic thought is currently the predominant thought process among humans.

tenets of autotheism. Hinduism and Buddhism are considered to have about one billion, six hundred million followers, although not all branches of those two religions would be considered autotheistic.

Value-judgment theisms include eutheism, the belief that deities are only benevolent; dystheism, the belief that a deity is not wholly good and is possibly evil; maltheism, a deity exists but is totally malicious; misotheism, active hatred for all god or gods. Eutheists would probably be listed among the nonaffiliated, while the other three categories, at least by most humans, would likely be considered atheists.

Theistic thought is not, as I suspect many of you believed it to be, a monolithic phenomenon in which almost everybody participates.

Atheism. Is atheism a bad word? According to George Carlin,[68] there are "no bad words ... [implied, by tone of voice, "there are"] bad thoughts, bad intentions." Is atheism a bad thought? If you consider the answer to be yes, why do you think atheism is a bad thought? Do you think quantum entanglement is a bad thought? If I suggested to you that quantum entanglement could be used to describe the manner in which the universe, and therefore the earth, was created, would that cause you to think that the term *quantum entanglement* was a bad thought? To a large degree, our immediate reaction to any word or thought is determined by our unconscious bias about how we look at the world. If you are a believer, you have a predetermined and unconscious but generally culturally acceptable (but not necessarily reasonable) view of the word *atheism*.

Atheism, as a process of thought, could not have existed without the presence of theistic thought. A version of that idea is the major premise of Michael J. Buckley in *At the Origins of Modern Atheism*.[69] He pursues that thought even further in *Denying and Disclosing God. The Ambiguous Progress of Modern Atheism,*[70] wherein he claims that by the latter half of the nineteenth century, humanism, which had largely up to that time been theistic, generated its own negation—its antitheism. Thus, he is claiming that antitheism and atheism are the same. He reaches that conclusion from a theistic stance. Buckley was a Jesuit priest and therefore a theist. While he is very diligent in his research and writing about the history of atheism, it appears that, in the long run, his theistic bias prevented him from being able to discern the difference between atheism and antitheism.

Is there a difference between the two? From a literal standpoint, atheism would have to mean opposition to an actual entity. Since god is only an idea confabulated by humans, atheism, as it is culturally understood currently, is not possible. One cannot oppose something that does not exist. Opposing an idea is not the same as opposing a reality. Biological humanists do not support the idea of god, since that confabulation is not a premise supported by the current status of human thought. Biological humanists are nontheists, and possibly even antitheists, but not atheists, in the context in which the term is currently culturally understood.

At the time the word *atheist* was introduced, the prevailing cultural presumption was that god was an actual being. The word implied not being in opposition to the idea of god but being opposed to an actual, existing being. That basic meaning still prevails. Since god is not an actual being but only an idea confabulated to explain an unknown phenomenon, being an atheist is being one who opposes an idea, not an actual being. You may still think being an atheist is a bad idea, but *atheist* is not a bad word.

Why *biological* humanism? The term *biological humanism* is a redundancy. Since humans are emergent biological beings, the term *biological* is implied in the word human. So, why add *biological* to the term *humanism*? Earlier when considering the history of the term *humanism*, we discovered that while the basic concept of humanism as a phenomenon of activity in which humans attempt to live together mutually to the benefit of all has existed since humans began to live together in groups, the phenomenon has never, in historical time, been a predominant mode of thought. It has waxed and waned in response to various social and cultural settings but, even currently, is not a predominant concept among humans. Why?

As suggested earlier, a conjunction between a changed view of authority, supported, if not caused, by the introduction of theistic thought, led to the development of a cultural bias in favor of the idea of god instead of human mutualism as the predominant mode of thought about the nature of human existence. Subsequent to this cultural change, all attempts to support humanism have proceeded from the premise that society in general understands what it means to be human. Particularly, in the last 150 years, because of advances in the fields of biology and archaeology, our understanding of the nature of humans as biological beings, rather than special beings created by a deity, has expanded exponentially. We are in a position currently to know that we are first emergent biological beings and subsequently humans. As a society of humans, we need to begin to put the emphasis on the proper syllable, rather than continuing to place the em-PHA-sis on the wrong syl-LA-ble. To help humanism totally arise from the sleeping beauty state, we need to emphasize that we are *biological* first and human secondarily. We are biological humanists.

Chapter 6

How Biological Humanism Can Replace the Idea of God

Viable faiths [religions] of the future
will be nontheistic and will not
deify either person or state.[1]

We only create a sense of good and evil as
well as norms of conscionable behavior
once we know about our own nature.[2]

The degree to which we cooperate sets
us apart from the rest of creation.[3]

Whatever happens, our capacity for
muscular bonding will not disappear.[4]

Humans first confabulated the idea of god about fifty thousand years ago. For about 300,950 years of nontheistic thought, human society operated on the principle of a mode of thought or action in which human interests and values predominate—a humanistic principle. To begin consideration of how biological humanism can replace the idea of god, I propose a counterfactual thought experiment:[5] what would be the nature of human society if humans had not confabulated the idea of god? While I will not attempt a complete description of a society without the idea of god, several major premises will be examined.

War[6] would not exist. The oldest archaeological site discovered of what possibly was a prehistoric massacre was found in a cemetery in northern Sudan. The cemetery contained a large number of skeletons dated approximately thirteen to fourteen thousand years old. Almost half of the skeletons had arrowheads embedded, possibly indicating they were casualties of warfare. Those circumstances would place the first record of warfare in humans as having existed after humans had confabulated the idea of god.

The absence of war does not mean the absence of violence between individuals or even the absence of intergroup violence. Raymond Kelly[7] explains that war results from a societal conceptual transition from individual assault for cause to assault on any member of a group as assault for cause. Gat Azar[8] concurs with that definition.

Recall the discussion of the relationship between authority and deism in the last chapter. Authority, before society came under the influence of deism, precluded the use of external means of coercion. It is inconceivable, to me, that a society without a belief in the use of external means of coercion as acceptable could arrive at the definition of war cited above. Without the introduction of theistic thought, the concept of war would not have been possible.

Consider some of the advantages of a society without war. The governments of the world currently spend about $20 billion annually for military budgets.[9] Think of all the improvements in human welfare that could accrue worldwide if we lived in a society without war.

Slavery[10] would not have existed. The practice of slavery depends on the concept of ownership of property. The earliest evidence of the existence of slavery was in China between the eighteenth through twelfth century BCE. Slavery was rare among gatherer-hunter societies and only became prevalent following the invention of agriculture and a settled way of life. Had humans not confabulated the idea of god, the terrible scourge of slavery would have been avoided.

The Crusades would not have occurred. The Crusades[11] were only possible because society had accepted the concept of war as well as having transformed the concept of authority as the right of a societal entity to exercise force. The societal entity responsible for the Crusades was a theistic entity, the Catholic Church. A theological basis for a just war was established by Augustine (354–430 CE), if the war was proclaimed by a legitimate authority, was defensive or for the recovery of lands, and did not involve an excessive (not defined) degree of violence.

When the first Crusade was announced by Pope Urban II in 1095 CE, volunteers were required to take a public vow to be able to join the crusade. Historians consider that the prospect of mass ascension into heaven at Jerusalem was a major motivating factor for volunteers. Certainly, participants were promised absolution for their sins for participation.

During the second Crusade, which began in 1146 CE, anti-semitic preaching by a Cistercian monk caused extensive massacres of Jews. Arguably, the Crusades were the origin of much conflict that still exists in many portions of the world.

Humanism would prevail. One cannot say with absolute certainty that humanism would be the predominant philosophical view if theism had not developed and that none of the above considered phenomena would have developed. However, given the extended period of time which humanism preexisted theistic thought, and the implications of the influence of theistic thought on cultural phenomena subsequent to its development, the premise of the continued existence of humanism and its influences is not unwarranted. Imagining a world where humanism prevails is a potentially highly productive idea for humans. The results of the thought experiment suggest that a nontheistic society would be preferable to a theistic society.

Are belief in god and religion the same? Many, if not most, think the answer to that question is yes. Are the two phenomena inextricably related? In the opening epigram at the beginning of the chapter, I suggested replacing the author's word *faiths* with the word *religions*. Can a phenomenon that is nontheistic be called a religion? What is a religion; or, what is religion? Possibly, the most comprehensive definition of religion is "a construct invented to describe a feeling, prompted by ritual, which became associated with the idea of god."

In the prevailing cultural view, particularly in the United States, your answer to the question "What is religion?" will be biased by the association you have with your particular religious organization. That stance is certainly the opinion of Brent Nongbri in *Before Religion: A History of a Modern Concept*,[12] where he says that religion is anything that sufficiently resembles modern Protestant Christianity. One might think that his title suggests that religion is only a modern concept. He is using modern[13] to refer to the postclassical period that began about 1500 CE. To support his point, he traces, linguistically, the origin and usage of the word religion. In ancient Greek, the word *treskeia,* which became *religio* in Latin and religion in English, was used by the Greek historian Herohotus to mean something like "ritual." This meaning of *rite* or *ritual* persisted for centuries (more about this later).

Ancient Hebrew and Aramaic did not have a word that is routinely translated in modern languages as religion. Prior to the twentieth century, the English word religion had no direct equivalent in Arabic. In a 1649 translation of the Qur'an, the term *law* was translated "religion," and in a 2003 translation, *law* was translated "faith."

Wilfred Cantwell Smith[14] attempted to answer the question "What is religion?" He concluded that the term religion was confusing, unnecessary, and distorting, so much so that he suggested that the term should be abandoned. However, in suggesting a replacement phenomenon for religion, he recommended a pattern of behavior that would be consistent with humanism, although he did not use the term *humanism* in describing his recommended phenomenon.

Only in the last four to five hundred years did the word religion come to mean what it is generally considered to mean currently. To most people, their view of what constitutes religion is determined only by their personal experience.

Another way to approach this issue would be to ask, "How do you know you are religious?" In many religious traditions, particularly Christian Protestantism, the answer might be, "I feel I have a personal relationship with Jesus Christ." That answer, obviously, would not be the answer of millions of other people who consider themselves religious. Therefore, since most of you probably would admit that at least some people who are not Christians are religious, then something additional must also be present in what makes you religious. What then is the something else that defines religion?

Previously, in considering the nature of theism, we discovered that not all religions are theistic. Therefore, not even believing in the idea of god is what allows one to be an adherent of a religion, or religious. What then is the unifying element among all religions that makes them a religion? From an anthropological standpoint, that element is ritual.[15] But some of you are thinking, *We don't have rituals in my religious tradition*. Here again, some of us fall prey to the short-term view phenomenon, which is highly prevalent in current, particularly Western, culture.

What is ritual? Dictionary.com[16] displays seven definitions focused on religion or religious activities before finally presenting two additional ones that more nearly approximate the original meaning of the term ritual: "any practice or pattern of behavior regularly performed in a set manner." At the end of the first definition given, "an established or prescribed procedure for a religious or other rite," the term *rite* is highlighted. By following the highlighted hint, one again finds four definitions focusing on religion before reaching the last definition, "any customary observance or practice."

Essentially, the definition of ritual is "patterned, repetitive, motion." From an anthropological perspective,

> Ritual is a common form of animal behavior ... [which has] become religious as it has been rationalized and explained in language by reference to beliefs about supernatural beings. ... religion can be defined as the use of language to increase the effectiveness of ritual.[17]

Ritual existed in animals millions of years before humans confabulated and developed the idea of god and invented religion. Geza Teleki[18] describes a "rain dance" by a troop of chimpanzees in the wild. During a heavy rain, the troop plodded up a steep slope toward a ridge at the top. At a large clap of thunder, a big male stood upright and swayed and swaggered rhythmically from foot to foot as his pant-hoots rose above the sounds of the rain beating down. Several others joined in while younger chimpanzees watched from the treetops. The performance lasted about twenty minutes. He also reported that similar ritualistic activities occurred when the chimpanzees considered a situation potentially dangerous. Many other ethnologists report similar ritualistic activities among a variety of animals. Because of the significance of motion in the development and continuation of living organisms, including humans, we have an extremely long-lived dependence on patterned, repetitive motion—ritual.

In ancient Roman culture,[19] the essence of religion was strict observance and proper performance of ritual. Contrary to what many of you probably think, religion is an add-on to ritual, rather than the other way around.

What, then, is ritual? Recall our consideration in chapter 3 of biases and how they develop, partially because action precedes thought and because of our biological inclination toward repetitive action, which tends toward the development of habits.* Those concepts provide the *biological* foundations in humans for our understanding of ritual as the central focus of what we call religion. The *cultural* foundations for ritual have a similar background in animals. Rituals were used by other animals to efficiently perform intricate individual and social behaviors involved in combat, food gathering, and reproduction. Rituals served that same purpose for early humans.[20] When humans confabulated the idea of god, dependence on ritual was well established

* For further consideration of "habit," see the Metalogue, "What Is a Habit?" in appendix A.

and eventually was transferred to activities associated with the idea of god.

Roy A. Rappaport, in *Ritual and Religion in the Making of Humanity,*[21] concurs in this approach. In defining ritual, he says that his definition encompasses not only human rituals but also stylized displays reported by ethnologists as occurring among birds, animals, and even insects. As an example, he cites that just as faithful members of a certain church congregate at the appointed time for services on Sunday, so starlings or grackles congregate at a certain specific location at dusk. Further, he says that religion originates from ritual so defined and that ritual is a social act that is basic to humanity.

What is the purpose of ritual in religion? According to Rappaport, ritual allows the participants to convey to themselves and to other participants information about their own physical, psychic, or social states—that is, feelings. Perhaps, he says, that is the only purpose.

What then is the relationship between ritual and religion? Religion is a construct invented by humans to describe a feeling, prompted by ritual, which became associated with the idea of god. The sequence is, therefore, this: as biological beings, we have an innate dependence on motion, which developed into patterned, repetitive activities (rituals), which we learned to use to display our feelings to ourselves and others, which, when we confabulated the idea of god, we applied to that idea, thereby creating religion. We then carefully teach the end result without explaining the background causes and development and call the effect "religious conversion."

For biological humanism to replace the idea of god, it must be able to serve the function that religion currently serves. As religion is a construct invented by humans to describe a feeling that is prompted by ritual, if biological humanism can accommodate ritual, it can serve as a religion. On this front, biological humanism is far ahead of any existing religion. As considered previously, ritual arose from our biological inclination toward repetitive action. Biological humanism is tailor-made for ritual and, therefore, religion.

What values does religion provide? In the Christian tradition, the one with which I am the most familiar, the Bible begins by telling how the world was created. Only the most strictly literalist believers think the world was actually created in six days. The rationalizations to make that belief viable are numerous but largely, thoroughly unconvincing. Geologists' ability to date the age of the earth is generally accepted, as is some version of something like the big bang theory of how the universe was created. Biological humanists would find those positions acceptable.

By way of the creation stories, religion tells humans who they are—special creations of god. With its emphasis on human life as an emergent, complex, nonlinear phenomenon, the creation story for biological humanists would be "life emerges at the edge of chaos,[22] prompted by quantum entanglement."* The question of who we are and the importance of that question have been previously considered. The point here is that biological humanism, as a religion, provides a functional explanation of who we are as humans.

Religion traditionally tells humans how we should behave. Humanism historically has done likewise. Frequently, at least in the Christian tradition, when asked how one should treat one another, the golden rule[23] is cited as guidance. This ethic of reciprocity appeared at least as early as 2040 BCE and most assuredly existed in oral transmission

* The phrase "prompted by quantum entanglement" is my personal addition to an otherwise well-established phenomenon.

long before that. The concept of authority considered previously depended on such a concept.

The ethic of cooperation, as opposed to conflict, has long been a basic premise of biological humanism. As indicated in chapter 1, cooperation may even be a biological imperative. Certainly, according to the third epigram at the beginning of the chapter, cooperation is a major component of what it means to be human. Consider also the discussion about war at the beginning of this chapter. Humanism always has, and biological humanism always will, foster cooperation over conflict as an ethical premise for humans. Biological humanism, as a religion, will provide the guidance necessary for helping us as humans know how to treat one another.

Religions generally, and the Christian religion particularly, tell us of our future after we die. The Christian religion particularly predicts a glorious future life for the faithful and a perilous, pitiful future for the unfaithful. Not unlike the creation story, these premises are fraught with difficulties that can only be overcome with extreme rationalizations and contradictions with reality.

This thought experiment demonstrates the problem just described.

A Puzzlement for the Religious

A righteous, young woman was married at fifteen years. She and her husband lived happily, faithfully, and righteously together until the husband died in the fifty-third year of their marriage. The woman grieved the death of her husband for two years. Then she married another righteous man, and they lived happily, faithfully, and righteously until he died five years later. The woman again grieved the death of her husband for two years, after which she married for the third time. She and her new husband lived together happily, faithfully, and righteously for twenty years. They both died peacefully in their sleep on the same night. The woman went to heaven, where she met all three of her husbands. How will the woman decide which husband with whom she should spend eternity?

Biological humanism avoids the dilemma posed in this situation. As biological beings, when life ends, we end. This knowledge allows us to focus on the importance of the time we have to live. Contemplation of that consideration allows us to have a greater focus on the opportunities and responsibilities we have to ourselves and to one another as humans. As Damasio says in the second epigram at the beginning of the chapter, since biological humanism tells us who we actually are, we will now be able to create a sense of good and evil and norms of conscionable behavior. Biological humanism as a religion affords significant, important guidance about how we should live together as humans.

What would biological humanism as a religion be like? Ritual would be a central focus. In many existing religious traditions, recitation of a creed is a common ritualistic activity, so much so that Dictionary.com, following the tradition of displaying as the first definition the prevailing current usage, defines creed[24] as "any system, doctrine, or formula of religious belief, as of a denomination," followed by "any system or codification of belief or of opinion." Existing humanistic organizations frequently avoid references to a creed,[25] probably because historically creeds came to be considered authoritatively imposed instead of voluntarily accepted and recited.

Creeds, in the more generic sense, are abundant in society. Many creeds are affiliated with secular rather than religious activities. In the United States, the Pledge of Allegiance[26] is an example of a creed that was originally humanistic and later changed to have a theistic emphasis. The original form of the pledge was written in 1892 and adopted by Congress as the pledge in 1942. The official name, the Pledge of Allegiance, was adopted in 1945. The words "under God" were added in 1954. (I grew up reciting the Pledge of Allegiance before the words "under God" were added.)

Numerous other organizations in the United States, particularly military organizations, have creeds:[27] the Rifleman's Creed is an unofficial creed of the United States Marine Corps; the Ranger Creed is the official creed of the US Army Rangers; the US soldiers creed is a set of values and morals that all US Army personnel are encouraged to live by; the Sailor's Creed is the official creed of the United States Navy; the Airman's Creed is the official creed of the United States Air Force; the United States Postal Service has an unofficial creed.

"The American's Creed"[28] is the title of a resolution passed in the United States House of Representatives on April 3, 1918. It generally reflects many of the principles originally formulated by Thomas Jefferson in the Declaration of Independence but concludes with a short paragraph:

> I therefore believe it is my duty to my country to love it, to support its constitution, to obey its laws, to respect its flag, and to defend it against all enemies.

Evidently, the resolution was intended to counter some of the objection to the draft instituted to support the United States effort in World War I, as it has received little public attention since that time.

What is the purpose of a creed? A creed, particularly when recited in a ritualistic setting, allows one to affirm, publicly, association with others in a common endeavor or enterprise. Creeds usually identify the nature of the association to which the participants belong and in some fashion identify the nature of the endeavor or enterprise and the behavior expected of the participants. Benefits of participation are generally implied.

I propose the following creed for biological humanism: "For the strength afforded by close association with other biological entities, we are truly grateful." Does this statement meet the criteria for a creed? The phrase "with other biological entities" is a multifaceted phrase. It identifies the reciter as a biological entity, thereby proclaiming all participants as fellow biological entities. The word "other" is also multifaceted. It claims human association with other nonhuman biological entities, thereby recalling the billions of year history of humans. By implication, it denies our having been specially created by god, thereby claiming a biological, and eventually humanistic, nature of the participant. The entire phrase identifies who the participants are and what their association is with one another and other biological entities.

The phrase "for the strength afforded by close association" suggests the appropriation of a feeling. "Closeness" can mean simply being crowded; however, in general parlance, it usually means nearness and possibly affectionate nearness. Being crowded usually suggests being uncomfortable. The meaning intended here is more like the feeling of affection for a close friend or for a pet or other animal that you appreciate. That kind of closeness usually does make one feel stronger.

As I write, our country, indeed the world, is suffering the onslaught of the corona virus. The airways are replete with statements from all quarters about "how we are all in this together," and occasional conversations even suggest that we may be made stronger because of our having to endure the effects of this situation. I suggest that all of those statements are prompted by a feeling of "the strength afforded by close association with other biological entities." Humans generally are aware of this phenomenon, even if they have never personally attached a descriptive phrase to it. Our humanness and the ancient association with other biological entities is what makes this feeling possible. All of these concepts are implied in that short phrase.

The phrase also implies a spirit of cooperation. One may feel close to a competitor, but usually one feels closer to a cooperator. As suggested in the third epigram at the beginning of the chapter, cooperation is a very important component of our successful life as humans.

The phrase "we are truly grateful" suggests a feeling but also a state of being. Traditionally, in religious settings, being grateful implies being grateful to god. However, one may also be grateful to others; that is the meaning suggested here—we are grateful to one another for the strength we feel by our close association with one another and other biological entities. The proposed creed for biological humanism meets the usual criteria for a genuine creed.

How would the creed be used in biological humanism as a religion? Opportunities for the use of the creed are numerous. Eating in a group is an ancient tradition among humans. Almost assuredly, ritualistic practices accompanied group eating even before the idea of god was confabulated. With the confabulation of the idea of god, giving thanks to the gods for food acquired would have developed. Grace before meals is a common practice, so much so that most children are very early taught rhythmic graces. The humanistic creed easily substitutes as a ritualistic statement in that setting. Users of the creed would be aware that the gratitude being expressed was directed toward one another (and possibly even toward the biological entities who provided the substance for the meal) rather than toward god.

Frequently, in many public gatherings, an invocation is used to begin the event. In any situation in which an invocation is used, the humanistic creed could easily be used instead. Normally an invocation invokes the support of god for whatever activity is being conducted. Many activities (business, political, social, etc.) focus on the element of cooperation as being necessary in the endeavor being considered. Since cooperation is implied in the content of the creed, ritualistic recitation of the creed in those situations would be highly appropriate.

At a wide range of other activities in the United States, including political rallies and sporting events, the national anthem is sung at the beginning. Recently, a considerable amount of consternation has arisen over the stance taken by some participants, particularly at sporting events, to the singing of the national anthem. The humanistic creed, with its focus on unity and cooperation, would serve well as a replacement in those settings. I cannot imagine every situation in which recitation of the creed would be appropriate, but I cannot imagine any situation in which it would not be appropriate. All joint public settings could be seen as religious in a society in which biological humanism was the religion.

Repetitive motion is another important feature of ritual. William H. McNeill,[29] in his history of dance and drill, presents an extensive history of the importance of repetitive motion in human society. McNeill became interested in the topic as a result of his experience of marching in cadence in training for his service in World War II. He reports that his experience was mesmerizing and near trance producing. What he was feeling, of course, was the effect of the biological importance of motion in the development and continuation of life. His observations about the possible effects of the importance of maintaining that phenomenon are appropriate to our consideration here.

He pointed out that because feelings are inseparable from their gestural and muscular expression, various forms of dance have been prevalent in human society—tribal dances in older cultures and street dancing in more recent cultures. Further, he observed that humans have not yet quite managed to develop a thoroughly satisfying style of urban living. He suggested that the long-term viability of human civilization would require adjustments in human behavior in which keeping in time, a ritualistic activity, would be required. While he did not suggest specific activities, he said that the development of community activities that focused on joint muscular activity possibly would be able to replace the function previously performed by ritualistic dancing. He also suggested that it would be unwise to continue our contemporary disregard of this aspect of human society; hence his quotation in the fourth epigram at the beginning of the chapter.

How does this discussion relate to our consideration of humanism as a religion? Earlier I suggested that the creation story for biological humanism would be "life emerges at the edge of chaos prompted by quantum entanglement." The foundation for that concept is "motion is the essence of existence." In today's culture, at most activities designated as sporting events, most people in attendance are considered spectators. Spectators, as opposed to those performing the sport, are passive. While some ritualistic activity does occur among spectators, it might be possible to conceive ways in which to engage the spectators more actively, in some organized fashion, to allow spectatorship to perform the role that village dancing formally provided.

Both the establishment and use of the creed for biological

humanism and an emphasis on muscular (ritualistic) activities in public gatherings would place a significant emphasis on ritual and its place in biological humanism as a religion.

A close associate with ritual is *music*. Much music, and some of the most famous music in the world, has been written with religious themes. Almost assuredly, when biological humanism is established as the predominant form of human religion, it will acquire its own cadre of music. However, a song by Phil Ochs,[30] "When I'm Gone," will serve well as an initial anthem for biological humanism. The song magnificently presents one of the core principles of biological humanism—the immediacy of one's responsibility to one another:

> There's no place in this world where I'll be-
> long when I'm gone
> and I won't know the right from the wrong
> when I'm gone
> and you won't find me singin' on this song
> when I'm gone
> so I'll just have to do it while I'm here.*

The song continues for six stanzas, reporting different situations of human responsibility, ending each situation with the line, "I'll just have to do it while I'm here." The theme is not mournful; rather, it is uplifting and encouraging—the perfect milieu for an anthem for biological humanism.

A third focus for biological humanism as a religion will be establishing a *feeling* that biological humanism is a religion. Feelings do not come with an explanatory tag attached. Feelings are observed, explained, and taught. "We have

* The original of this line was "I guess I'll have to do it"—edited here for a more positive stance for a biological humanism anthem.

emotions first and feelings after[31] ... Consciousness must be present if feelings are to influence the subject having them beyond the immediate here and now."[32] An emotion occurs as a biological response to some circumstance; we become aware of that emotion—a feeling—and we explain to ourselves, or someone explains to us, what that feeling means. If the emotion-feeling recurs frequently enough, *we* put a tag on it. The meaning of feelings is learned.

Learning, by society in general, that biological humanism is a religion will not be easy. First we will have to unlearn the current belief that religion is absolutely connected with the idea of god. We do that, in part, by learning that the feeling that we called *religious* when we thought about god had been learned. When we *really* learn that, we can then learn that biological humanism can be a religion. We will then be able to associate the feeling that we have about the association between god and religion with the association between biological humanism and religion. While that may sound like an impossible task, I assure you it not only is possible but both liberating and uplifting when it occurs.

When society in general learns that biological humanism is a valid religion and the ritualistic activities described above are implemented, biological humanism can become the predominant form of religion. Theistic religion, with its focus on supernaturalism, is no longer tenable and viable. Humanity needs to abandon the idea of god and allow the sleeping beauty of (biological) humanism to fully and permanently awake.

Chapter 7

Why We Need to Abandon the Idea of God

The world population is projected to increase by 3.5 billion by the end of the century.[1]

Human society faces several significant problems in the near future. Large population growth is one such problem. Although recent scientific and technological advances provide means and opportunity to meet many of those problems, our collective attitude toward such advances will determine how effectively they may be used. While we eagerly embrace many new technological devices, for example, cell phones, many others meet significant opposition, at least in some quarters.

One can hardly buy any food product these days that does not contain a label claiming "non GMO." Genetically modified organisms[2] are simply organisms modified by humans in a fashion occurring naturally. *You* are a naturally genetically modified organism. The egg and sperm from which your body developed came from two separate organisms. The combination of genetic material from those two organisms produced a new genetic component that became you.

Hybridization of plants and animals has existed at least as long as the beginning of agriculture. Almost any food product, animal or plant, that you consume regularly has undergone some form of hybridization. Humans performed the hybridization, in many instances (hybridization does also occur naturally without human interference). Genetic modification is a naturally occurring, useful phenomenon.

Why then all the fuss about genetic engineering?[3] I suggest that it is belief in god that is the cause for concern over genetic modification by humans. On the assumption that god created all organisms as they currently exist, genetic modification would be an insult to, and violation of, god's will and, therefore, objectionable. That premise carries over to numerous other scientific and technological phenomena, considered below.

In *The Global Food Crisis and What We Can Do to Avoid It,* Julian Cribb[4] begins with a story about the 2008 meeting of the G8 in Japan. He describes in detail the sumptuous banquet served at the meeting, with numerous courses and exotic dishes. He reports that the cost of that G8 meeting (not the banquet alone) was $500 million. A major topic at the meeting was the extreme famine conditions currently existing in many parts of the world. He says that the amount of money spent for the meeting could have fed one hundred million hungry children around the world. The causes of that immediate food crisis were considered to be numerous, but lack of adequate production (sometimes aggravated by complex economic issues, including inflation followed by a prolonged recession) was a central issue.

This incident highlights a number of problems for humanity but two in particular: the lack of awareness by much of human society of the living conditions of other fellow humans and a lack of concern for the mutual responsibility we share for the welfare of one another. Each of those lacks represents, what would be in humanistic terms, breaches of ethics.

Discussions at the G8 indicated that, as serious as the current food situation is, it would continue to increase at least until the middle of the twenty-first century. Considering the projected population increase by the end of the twenty-first century, possibly, the severity of the food crisis may have been underestimated.

In light of the severity of this problem, human society needs to be able to, without the interference of theistic biases, seriously consider ways to advance the development of foodstuffs, including, if possible, genetically modified foodstuffs.

A number of the problems facing human society might be classified under the general heading "global warming." Jeff Goodell[5] highlights one of those problems in *The Water Will Come: Rising Seas, Sinking Cities and the Remaking of the Civilized World.* He begins with a fictitious report of a hurricane in Miami in 2037. The winds were 175 mph. Most buildings were removed from their foundations. A foot of sand was deposited in many locations. A seventeen-mile stretch of highway between Miami and Fort Lauderdale disappeared into the ocean. The local wastewater treatment plant became inoperable, requiring the city to dump tons of raw sewage into the ocean. The remaining beaches became strewn with the effects of that dumping. The ocean waters caused shortages in the underground electrical supply, and much of the area was without power for months. While politicians claimed that "Miami would be back," it was obvious to local residents that the city was doomed.

Goodell reports that he had the idea for this opening to the book after having personally visited an area in New York City in 2012 after Hurricane Sandy occurred. While the conditions he observed were not quite as severe as those in the scenario he conjured for the opening to the book, the results were just as devastating. Streets were littered with debris and garbage; water stains remained on windows in buildings four to five feet from floor level; what recovery was possible took weeks.

Throughout the remainder of the book, he reports current situations around the world in which rising waters are already displacing individuals and sometimes entire communities. The basic cause of rising oceans is considered to be melting of glaciers, caused by excessive emissions of carbon dioxide into the atmosphere. At the current rate of emissions, the oceans are projected to rise between four to thirteen feet by the end of the century. Imagine the displacement of currently settled communities that would cause.

Rising temperatures is also considered a result of global warming. Goodell[6] also writes about that problem. Paul Crutzen,[7] who was a signatory of the humanist manifesto of 2003, is an atmospheric chemist who is best known for his work on ozone depletion, for which he received a Nobel Prize in 1995. He was also one of the originators of the term *Anthropocene*, to indicate a period in which human activity began to affect climate conditions.

In the same year (2006) that Al Gore[8] began his quest to encourage the world's citizens to help personally in reducing carbon dioxide emissions, Crutzen suggested geoengineering as a means of reducing carbon dioxide emissions, because personal effort reduction had not been highly successful in the past ten years. Geoengineering, while technically feasible, seemed a bit counterintuitive. The idea entailed placement of reflective particles into the stratosphere to provide a kind of shade for the earth, thereby reducing the temperature. The premise for the idea originated from the realization from atmospheric studies of the past that indicated the emission of volcanic ash had caused cooling of the planet. Because, however, prior climate control efforts focused on the elimination of substances from the atmosphere, the suggestion of adding substances, even though research had shown that something similar had worked in the past, seemed possibly unrealistic. Although no significant efforts have been pursued about the idea, the point in our consideration here is that humans are capable of conceiving potential solutions to problems associated with climate control and, therefore, possibly giving assistance to other problematic areas. Society needs constructs for examining proposed solutions that are deemed acceptable and useful, and a biological humanistic setting, rather than a theistic setting, so that the effects of those proposed solutions may be considered readily and reasonably rather than hindered or shackled by theistic biases.

Jane Metcalfe,[9] founder of Neo.Life, in a publication containing twenty-five visions for the future of our species, suggests that "humans now have the tools to intervene in our own evolution and build a better world." Each of the twenty-five presentations suggests approaches that could potentially dramatically improve the nature of human existence. Many focus on some of the issues previously discussed in this chapter. One even discusses a possibility that might be of interest to theists—how to maintain the essence of your life after you die.

She and some of the other scientists whose ideas are presented in the book developed a rough draft of a manifesto for the future of Homo sapiens. The manifesto is worth your consideration. For such enterprises to be considered seriously, and for the overall welfare of humanity, we need to abandon the idea of god and fully embrace biological humanism.

Postscript

Personal Notes

By the title to this postscript, I do not intend to imply that what I have written previously is not personal—it is very personal. Here I want to describe how I came to realize that I was a biological humanist. I was born in 1935 in the middle of the Great Depression. My father was a sharecropper on a small cotton farm. He worked on the farm in association with a businessman in the town about a mile from the farm. He had a third-grade education. My mother had an eighth-grade education.

When I was old enough, I worked on the farm, helping with the animals and sometimes working in the fields. My father and his associate lost the farm, and we moved to a small rural town of about 1,600 people when I was about eleven years of age. The high school I attended was small; we had twenty-one members in my graduating class. In my late preteens, I began attending the Methodist church in that community. I attended the youth group meetings, attended worship services, and eventually began to sing in the choir. I was baptized and became a member of the Methodist Church. I was taught to believe that god speaks to people to help direct them in their life. I believed it.

The mother of my father's farming associate frequently attended the church I attended. When I was in my early teens, she told me that she thought I had ministerial tendencies. I can't recall that she made much of an impression on me at the time; however, much later, I did remember that conversation.

When I graduated high school, I planned to go to college. My older brother (five years older than I) had graduated from college, and I wanted to also. After moving to town, my father began operating small businesses, and I worked for him at those various businesses. He allowed me to keep the money I made so that when I graduated from high school, I had saved enough money for tuition at a small liberal arts college sponsored by the Methodist Church in a town about seventy miles away.

While in high school, I had played football and really enjoyed it. I was selected by the coach to help coach a group of junior high football players and enjoyed that experience. When I was deciding what career path to pursue in college, coaching was high on my list of considerations. However, although I don't remember realizing it at the time, the conversation in which the lady suggested that I might have ministerial tendencies must have influenced me more than I realized, because in preparing for college, I decided to prepare for the pastoral ministry.

At that time in the Methodist Church, a prospective minister had to appear before the governing body of their local church and answer the question, "Do you believe you have been called to preach?" My answer to the board was yes. I believed it. When I enrolled in college, I chose English as my major because I had a very good English teacher in high school and enjoyed the subject greatly. Because I had grown up on a farm and had an interest in animals and plants, and although I had only two classes in high school that were in any way related to science, I chose biology as my minor. Biology, in that school in that time, had a broad sweep. I took a biology class almost every semester in college because the biology teacher was excellent and I found the material fascinating. The course in evolution was an eye-opener, as was genetics (strictly Mendelian genetics; DNA had been discovered but had not yet made it into textbooks). I was probably the only ministerial student in that college who took more than simply the required course in biology.

In my English classes, I had a class in Milton, where I wrote a paper comparing the view of hell in Milton's *Paradise Lost* with those in Dante's *Inferno*. I came away convinced that something was not quite right with that concept. Not long after that (I'm not sure how long), I decided that hell could not be a proper concept.

About the middle of my sophomore year in college, I was offered the responsibility of student pastor of a circuit of four churches about twenty miles away from the town in which I grew up. I was married the middle of my junior year and in the following summer was transferred to another four-circuit charge in a town about forty-five miles from the college I was attending. I was responsible for full pastoral duties in addition to attending college. With responsibility for four churches, each church had one morning and one evening service per month. In the summers, when school was not in session, I arranged to have at least one service per week in each of those churches.

Upon graduation from college, I enrolled in divinity school at Vanderbilt University. For our consideration here, the most pertinent thing I learned in classes in divinity school was the application of the principles of higher criticism to the Bible. Church history and history of doctrine were also revealing but not so much as discovering, for example, the very close parallels of the wording of the Gospels, the realization that not all of Paul's letters were probably written by Paul, that the first five books of the Old Testament were a compilation of four different writers (or groups of writers), and so on. I came to view the Bible not only as a book of religious inspiration but a book to be read critically. The Word of God certainly was not the words of god.

I graduated from divinity school in 1960, was ordained an elder, and was appointed to a two-church circuit that summer. With no time required for school, I began to read more widely than I ever had before. I wrote a letter to the editor of a magazine published for Methodist ministers in response to an article that had been published and was asked my permission to have the letter published. In 1963, the week in which John F. Kennedy was assassinated, I was appointed to a single church in a small town about twenty-five miles from where I grew up.

I served as the pastor of that congregation for the next four and a half years. For the first time in my career, I was responsible for preparing two sermons a week. To make sermon planning easier, and because Paul's letter to the Romans has such significance historically, I chose to build my sermons on that letter for the evening services. It took about four years to finish that series of sermons. I also began to read even more widely. One of the books I read during that time was Wallace's *Religion. An Anthropological View.* I remember being very impressed with the book but was surprised about how much I didn't remember when I started using it for research for this book. I worked diligently at the role of being a pastoral minister and felt very appreciated by the members of my congregations.

During the time of this appointment, a number of us who had graduated both college and divinity school together decided to have an occasional reading seminar at the college from which we had graduated. At one of our meetings, we read *The Phenomenon of Man* by Pierre Teilhard de Chardin. I invited my biology teacher, who I knew taught a weekly Sunday school class at a nearby Methodist Church, to read the book and attend with us, which he did. Everyone present (except the biology teacher) had the same theological training that I had, but no one except the biology teacher and I realized that the book was more theological than scientific. De Chardin was a Jesuit priest who was trained as a paleontologist and geologist. But he *was* a Jesuit priest. However, because of the scientific language in the book and the lack of exposure to scientific material by the remainder of the group, even though they were trained to read theological material, they were blinded by the scientific language. I was a bit distraught. My fellow ministers were responsible for congregations, many of which had or would have sophisticated scientists among the membership. How would they be able to minister adequately to those people if they could not understand their language? That question stuck with me.

Meanwhile, I began to realize that I did not believe that Jesus had been raised from the dead. Biologically, dead people don't come back to life. I began to read very carefully all the accounts of the resurrection in the New Testament. I discovered something very interesting. In 1967, I wrote, because I could not afford not to, a paper (see appendix B) titled "Who Is Jesus?" Because at that point I still believed god was real, I concluded that Jesus could be an example and a teacher, but he did not rise from the dead. I also found myself thinking, as I distributed the elements of the Lord's supper, that I didn't believe the words I was saying: "This is my body; this is my blood." My scientific understanding was overriding my theological understanding. But still I felt that god was real and provided comfort for people and that I could assist them in understanding that.

The last year of that appointment was my seventh year since having been ordained. I would be eligible for a sabbatical year and decided to take it. No one that I knew of, since my association with that conference, had ever taken a sabbatical. No remuneration was available, but I decided to enroll at Iowa State University, get a master's degree, and possibly be able to get a job teaching in a theological school, classes about the relationship between science and religion. Only later did I discover that nobody cared. I sold dictionaries door to door during the summer, my wife took a job in Ames to support us during the school year, and I finished my master's degree in three quarters. About the middle of the last quarter, I contacted the conference about an appointment for the following year and was informed that since I was out of the loop, I would have to start at the beginning. Prior to enrolling at Iowa State, I had taken a civil service exam, thinking that I might be able to get a part-time civil service job while in school. That didn't work out. However, about the same time that I discovered my situation in the conference, I received the notice of a job interview with the Veterans Administration in Minneapolis. I went for the interview and was offered a job and accepted. I notified the conference of my intention to locate and asked the delegate to the conference from the last church I had served to read a statement on my behalf, which she did.

I worked for the Veterans Administration for twenty years and retired. I moved to Lubbock, Texas, and taught technical communications at Texas Tech University for eleven years. While working for the Veterans Administration, I became aware that veterans' hospitals employed chaplains. I thought the combination of my knowledge of Veterans Administration regulations and my experience in the ministry would be a useful match for hospitalized veterans. I investigated the matter and discovered that, to be eligible for a potential chaplain's job, I would need to be readmitted to a conference in the Methodist Church. No one was interested. When I moved to Lubbock, I inquired of the local Methodist hierarchy whether my teaching job at Texas Tech might qualify as an appointment in their conference (many ministers receive appointments to universities). I received no reply to my inquiries. Again, nobody cared.

Through working in the area of technical communications, I increased my ability to read complex technical materials. When I began to read, especially neuroscience materials, and began to understand how the brain works, I realized that my long-felt suspicions were more than just suspicions. But still I believed that god was real.

Recall the incident in chapter 2 about Magritte and the pipes: that was my eureka moment. In association with that understanding, I realized that it was not god who had called me to preach—it was Mrs. Annie Cronan, the mother of my father's farming associate. The idea of god was only something I had learned from others—not a real being.

I had known, at least since college, that I was a biological being. I knew about confabulation from having read neuroscience. I knew, generally, about social constructionism. But I did not connect the dots until viewing that painting. I was exhilarated. I was relieved. It was as much a conversion moment as any evangelical Christian can claim. I always had been a biological humanist—I just didn't know it till then!

Appendix A

I have an unpublished manuscript about how to understand and survive a verbally abusive relationship. In a verbally abusive relationship, both partners are victims: the person being abused is an abused victim; the abuser has a past that causes the abusive behavior and is, thus, a victim abuser; thereby the names of the participants in the metalogue. One of the techniques I use in the manuscript is presentation of a metalogue to assist in understanding complex phenomena. Gregory Bateson, in *Steps to an Ecology of Mind,*[1] invented the concept of metalogue and presents several as conversations between his daughter, Catherine, and himself. The metalogue that follows supplements the discussion of biases under consideration in the text.

METALOGUE: What is a Habit?

Abused Victim: What is a habit?

Victim Abuser: How old is your dictionary? Or, are you a Roman Catholic?

AV: Come on! Don't avoid the question; I'm serious, "What is a habit?"

VA: And I'm serious. I just happened to look up the meaning of "habit" the other day. I first used the old dictionary; you know, the one from the fifties, because it was handy. The first definition was "dress, garb, attire" especially of "a religions person," like a nun or priest. So I looked in the newer one and it said, "customary practice" for the first definition; "an acquired behavior pattern regularly followed until it has become almost involuntary," was number six and the one about religious dress was last, number twelve.

AV: How old was the second dictionary you used?

VA: Early seventies, I believe.

AV: So in about twenty years, the preferred usage almost completely reversed. That seems odd, because I seem to remember that in early health classes when we were learning about brushing our teeth we were told that we had to brush regularly until it became a habit. That would seem to be like the first or sixth definition in the newer dictionary.

VA: Which do you think is right?

AV: I'm not sure; the dictionaries are so confusing, but I guess I feel that the correct answer is the one about doing something until it becomes almost involuntary.

VA: I think so too because I keeping thinking, "Keep doing it until it becomes second nature," as what I remember. What made you ask about habits anyway?

AV: You always say that I say to you, "You're only doing that out of habit." I wondered what you thought I meant by that statement, and frankly, I wasn't sure what I meant either. So I thought we ought to talk about it. Besides, I was reading an article the other day that suggested that habits might be more the result of thought processes than actions.

VA: There you go again, bringing up thought or action. Next you'll be wanting to start talking about profanity again, and I thought we were finished with that topic. (For the metalogue about profanity between VA and AV, which occurred while they were still Partner 1 and Partner 2, instead of AV and VA, see Appendix IV).

AV: Although I'm not sure some form of habit isn't involved in the use of profanity, I'm content with our discussion about profanity, at least for now. Anyway, the article I was reading suggested that the way we were talked to as children probably helped determine what we thought about ourselves as adults, and therefore, helped determine, at least to a degree, what our actions are as adults.

VA: I'm not sure about all this stuff you read, but let's say for the moment that that is true. That doesn't seem consistent with the definitions we both grew up with. I'm not aware of anything which my parents said to me which makes me do any of the things you say I do from habit. If I'm not consciously doing an action how can I repeat it until it becomes almost involuntary? Can one <u>un</u>consciously act? That would be like a person in a coma doing something. Most of the people I've seen in a coma don't even move; some can't even breathe on their own.

AV: That raises an interesting point: what about breathing? Breathing was one of the actions adults talked about when explaining the meaning of habit; keep doing an action until it becomes second nature, like breathing. You mentioned that some people in a coma can't breathe on their own. Something else I read suggested that the limbic brain controls many of our automatic bodily functions, like breathing. So we don't learn to breathe; our brain just knows how to do it, and a number of other things, for us. So the example we learned as children, of doing an action until it became second nature, like breathing, wasn't a good example of a habit.

VA: I'm beginning to see why you asked what a habit is. We each thought of habits as being about the same thing, based on examples we learned as children. However, it seems that some of the examples, especially breathing, are not the result of learning, but something part of our brain just knows from the time we are born. And other things that may help us develop our habits, like things our parents said to us when we were children, even though we are not conscious of them now, help determine what our habits will be for the remainder of our lives.

AV: And habits may not be the result of conscious repetition of actions until they become almost unconscious actions on our part. They may be partially the result of actions and words of our parents, of which we are not now conscious, and cause us to unconsciously perform actions as adults.

VA: No wonder we have some bad habits; we don't even know we are going to have them and didn't directly develop some of them ourselves.

AV: There you go, saying one of those things you say from habit; taking every opportunity to blame someone else for something for which you are responsible.

VA: But....

AV: But, what?

VA: Nothing; go ahead.

AV: O. K. I don't think we get off the hook that easily. A part of the reason we develop the actions is probably things our parents said to us, but also partially because of our self-conversation, or explanatory style about what our parents said to us. It seems that we can and do change how we explain good things which happen, but the way we explain bad things which happen doesn't change, probably in our entire life or at least for 50 or so years of it.

VA: Seems as if we still have a lot to consider about habits.

AV: I agree. You mentioned "bad" habits. What about "good" habits? Do we acquire good habits in the same way we acquire some bad habits: at least partially from the actions of our parents?

VA: It would be nice to think that we ourselves learn the good habits but that what our parents say to us causes us to develop bad habits.

AV: You may think so, but I doubt if it works that way. I feel the cause of both good and bad habits is probably some of our own actions and some of what our parents say to us <u>and</u> what we say to ourselves about what they say to us. I just had an interesting thought: if we, in some way, learned our bad habits from what parents or other caregivers said to us as children (even though we may also have contributed somewhat to the process) could bad habits be unlearned?

VA: Probably so. One hears frequently about people who have lost their jobs having to be re-trained. That could mean that they just have to learn new skills, however. In training animals I'm pretty sure the trainers talk about having to help the animal <u>un</u>learn something that they have learned incorrectly so they can learn the correct way to do it. Some of animal training is very much like frequent repetition of an action until the animal learns to do it automatically on signal. That sounds like what we originally thought of as the way one develops habits. If relearning works for animals it would probably work for people too; that is, if we wanted to rid ourselves of a bad habit we'd have first to unlearn the bad habit and relearn a good habit to replace the bad one.

AV: I think you're right. In fact, I seem to remember that a type of psychotherapy called rational emotive behavior therapy (REBT) operates basically on that principle: through positive self-conversation (in REBT called self talk) one can erase a poor thought-action process and replace it with a good thought-action process. So, what have we discovered about habits?

VA: Well, first, I think we found that although we each had a similar idea of what a habit was and how we developed habits, based on what we had learned about habits early in our lives, what we learned was probably not entirely correct based on current thinking about habits and how they are developed.

AV: Yes, instead of being just repeating an action until it becomes almost automatic, the beginning development of habits may be based on ideas given us by parents and other caregivers very early in our lives and those ideas are reinforced, or possibly altered and solidified, by the things we say to ourselves about them through our explanatory style in our self-conversation, or self-talk, about them. That understanding, supplemented by repetitive action, becomes a habit.

VA: And I think we also concluded that bad habits possibly can be unlearned and replaced with good habits, possibly through a process of positive self-conversation and maybe a psychotherapeutic process of REBT, all which we're going to talk about later. I think this concept does explain some habits, especially those we have but aren't aware of, but how does this concept of habit relate to a conscious, direct action which becomes a habit, like brushing one's teeth?

AV: It seems to me that if one is treated well as an infant and a child and made to feel valued, when, as an older child or an adult, one determined to establish a habit of some activity, the establishment would be easier and more satisfying than if such pre-establishment activity had been absent.

VA: Yes, I also think that may be true. And I may have learned something else, but I'm going to reserve judgment on that until I think more about it.

Our partners suggest that things become habitual for us because of a combination of things: what we hear from others, especially our attachment figures; our self-conversation; and repetition of actions.

Appendix B

Who Is Jesus?

This paper may have been my first step toward realizing that I am a biological humanist, even though it was written 50 years ago. While I was unaware of how I could understand that god was not real, I had come to believe that Jesus was not the son of god and that he did not think so either. I have transcribed this paper from a copy of the original, just as I wrote it in 1967. (My apologies for my writing style in the '60's.)

Introduction

I. Traditional Views
II. Historically verifiable events in his life
III. A reconstruction on historical grounds
IV. The role of the Church based upon those views

Who is Jesus? The answer which one receives to this question will be determined by the person to whom it is directed. Ask it of a Moslem and he will say that he was a prophet from a line of prophets from whom Mohammed is descended. Ask it of a Jew you and he will say he is a very learned and unconventional interpreter of the Jewish law who lived in the first century. Ask it of an atheist and he will probably say that he is a man of whom ridiculous claims are made, or a rabble-rouser who got himself crucified in the first century because of his lack of political aptitude. Ask it of a Christian and he will say he is the Son of God.

"Who is Jesus?" is a question whose answer will depend upon the perspective from which one gives the answer rather than depending upon the person about whom the question is asked. Is this as it should be? Cannot the person speak for himself rather than having to have others speak for him, regardless of the perspective from which he speaks? It is my contention that he can and should speak for himself and that when he is allowed to do so, he becomes more valuable to everyone than is true when his worth is determined by the strength of the person or the religious tradition which tries to defend or explain him.

I.

Before we began to let Jesus speak for himself, it will be helpful to let his tradition speak for him. Since he is the person upon whom the Christian faith is built, let us first look at what this tradition claims for him – that he is the Son of God. The case for his being the Son of God is defended by choosing certain events in the gospels, the lives of Jesus of the New Testament. The basic events which are chosen for such a defense are usually these. Jesus was born to a young woman who was a virgin, one who had never had sexual intercourse with a man. His conception was therefore by miraculous power. God, through the Holy Spirit, caused a young woman named Mary to conceive. The Son she bore was Jesus, who was, from the very beginning of his earthly existence, the Son of God.

This Jesus, the Son of God, was so well recognized as such that God caused a new star to appear to announce his birth. This star was recognized by a group of men from another country who made the journey to visit this Son of God at the time of his birth. His birth was also announced by angels from heaven who sang in chorus of his birth to shepherds out in the fields near Bethlehem. This degree of miracle surrounded his birth.

The next item of his life which is recorded is at the age of 12 years, when he made his first journey to Jerusalem with his family for the temple services there for the feast of the passover. He remained in the temple, and because he was the miraculous Son of God, astounded the doctors of the law with his knowledge of the Jewish law and his questions concerning this law.

When the gospels next speak of Jesus he is a fully grown man who visits the camp of a wondering wilderness preacher named John the Baptist, who baptizes him. When he is baptized, though the accounts differ, each intends to present the fact that this Jesus is God's Son. From here he emerges as a wandering teacher who gathers a band of 12 followers about him. He deals magnificently with the Jewish law, yet in such a new way that the established religious authorities of the day object to many of his interpretations of the law. He not only teaches but amasses a reputation as a healer also. His healings run the gamut from the healing of a simple fever to raising people from the dead.

He finally arouses so much attention that he is accused of blasphemy by the Jewish leaders. These leaders persuade the Roman authorities that he is guilty of treason and insist that he be put to death. He is sentenced to death by Roman authorities, dies in a remarkably short time and is buried, late on the evening of the Jewish Sabbath. Early in the morning of the day after the Sabbath, a group of women go to anoint his body and find the stone rolled away. An angel tells them that the Jesus whom they seek is not there, but has risen from the dead. On several occasions the resurrected Jesus appears to various people: to Peter, to Mary Magdalene, to the disciples all at one time.

On the basis of this tradition the disciples begin to preach that this Jesus, whom God had raised from the dead, has become God's promised one, the Messiah, the Christ. From this time on he is no longer simply Jesus of Nazareth, but Jesus Christ, the Son of God.

And they add one other element to prove that this Jesus is the Son of God: his coming, death and resurrection has been predicted in the Scriptures of the old testament.

This, then, is the traditional case for Jesus of Nazareth, or the Divine Son of God. (1) God promised to send a savior (messiah) to his people through the predictions of the prophets. These prophets also predicted that this savior would not be accepted by the people, but would rather reject him and cause his death, and God would raise him from the dead. (2) Jesus of Nazareth was this promised savior. But in order to help prove his messiahship God had him conceived in a miraculous matter and born of the virgin Mary. In order to supplement this miraculous birth, the heavens themselves were disturbed in order to convince people of the divine nature of Jesus Christ. (3) In his youth his divinity showed in his unusual knowledge of the law. (4) In his ministry his divinity is proved by his miraculous power by his healings and, most finally, in the resurrection.

In a time when science was not developed and it was assumed that God might well act sporadically in unusual ways, this traditional view was accepted by almost anyone who might be exposed to it. But things are not this way now. Almost everyone knows that the world operates on a regular basis and not only our world but millions of other worlds also. The God who dips his finger down and sets aside the laws of nature, even for the purpose of convincing one of his love for them, is hardly acceptable. For one who understands his world as regularly operative and is confronted with the traditional view of Jesus stated above, what are the alternatives? He may decide that religion must fit into a separate category all its own, completely unrelated to the rest of life, and thus accept this religion and the Jesus who represents it. Or he would decide that it was all a lot of fabricated tales, and rejected it.

Either way he would lose. The Christian faith does have value and to reject it is to lose. But a Christian faith separated from the rest of life is not Christian faith and therefore one also loses. Are there any other alternatives?

II.

The problems which have been raised by the traditional view of Jesus are two. (1) In order to believe that he is the Son of God one must subscribe to a view of the world which is no longer acceptable to most people who think about their world. In other words, one is asked to accept a metaphysical system which can no longer be defended in order to believe in Jesus as the Christ. (2) Belief in Jesus as the Christ is not based, in the traditional view, upon a critical reading and comparing of all the records which we have about him. An alternative view of Jesus must take these two items into account.

Is it possible to present Jesus as the Christ within the context of the presently acceptable metaphysical view? It is not only possible, but necessary that one do so if he reads critically all the accounts which we have about Jesus.

The first problem which one faces in constructing an alternative view of Jesus is, "Did he really exist?". If the only source of our knowledge of Jesus was the New Testament we might write him off and be finished with the matter, because it is from some of the New Testament that the traditional view of Jesus arose. You will recall, however, that in the introduction it was mentioned that there are other groups of people besides Christians who make claims about Jesus also. The claims made by Jews and Moslems, which are religious claims also, do not contain supernatural claims which are metaphysically unacceptable to our time. Their claims about Jesus give credence to his existence as a normal human being.

The same is true of early historians. Eusebius, an early church historian, writes about Jesus as an existing person, as do others. There is no real problem in substantiating the claim that there was a historical person named Jesus of Nazareth.

The problem begins when one begins to go beyond that point. What does one do with the view that Jesus was conceived by the Holy Spirit in the womb of a virgin named Mary, and all the other supernatural, non-acceptable metaphysical events claimed to be associated with his birth?

Here one must begin his critical readings of the records. At first glance it seems a shame that no one other than adherents of the Christian religion wrote about the birth of this Jesus of Nazareth. But on second thought, the lack of writing about his birth is significant. What if one supposed that the stories of the new star, the visiting wise men from another country, the choir of angels who appeared to the shepherds were historical fact? Can one imagine that no one other than those who later were associated with faith in this Jesus would have been impressed enough by these spectacular events to remember something about them and later write them down? The fact that the stories, spectacular as they are, exist only in documents written to be propaganda leaflets for the faith indicate that one must at least ask some questions about their historical validity.

But there is a stronger argument than this one from the

faith documents themselves. In the New Testament there are two basic sources of information about Jesus of Nazareth. The most obvious one is the Gospels. The second is the writings of Paul. It is the Gospels with which one usually begins when he wants to find out something about Jesus. This is the first mistake. Biblical scholars have basically agreed that the following dates for events in the New Testament are generally correct. One can only say that the dates are generally correct because the records were not kept very carefully in those days.

The apostle Paul was the first person to write any of what is now the New Testament. The crucifixion of Jesus (about which we shall have more to say later) occurred about 27 or 28 AD. Paul wrote his first letters about 48 to 50 AD or about 20 years after the crucifixion. It is also significant to remember that Paul was not one of the original disciples who had been with Jesus during his lifetime. He became a Christian only after the crucifixion. He does his own writing about the things he considers important to the Christian faith. He never mentions the birth of Jesus, either by natural or supernatural means. If one were to have only the writings of Paul he would have no doctrine of the virgin birth with its accompanying metaphysical problems. This man, writing 20 years after the death of Jesus, says nothing about the spectacular events in the life of Jesus. Why? Obviously because he did not know anything about them. They did not exist at this time.

This view is also supported by the gospels, when looked at from a historical standpoint. The first gospel to be written was the gospel of Mark. Dates assigned to Mark differ, but the date somewhere between 60 and 70 AD, with the greater weight going to the latter date, is generally accepted. The gospel of Mark contains no stories about the birth of Jesus. It does make the claim that he is the Son of God in the opening verses, but it does not base its proof upon metaphysically unacceptable matters as a miraculous conception and a virgin birth, attended by new astronomical appearances and heavenly choirs. The first two, the oldest, sources of knowledge about Jesus in the New Testament do not base their claim for his being the Christ upon principles which are metaphysically unacceptable, at least in connection with Jesus' birth.

But what about the gospels of Matthew and Luke? It is generally agreed that the gospels of Matthew and Luke were written from about 80 to 90 AD with Matthew closer to 80 and Luke closer to 90. This means that they were this number of years removed from the birth of Jesus and 50 to 60 years removed from the death of Jesus. It means that they are also 30 to 40 years from Paul's writings and 10 to 20 years from Mark's gospel. From these dates, who would have been the more reliable writer from the historical point of view, given the fact that in that time much, even most, of the sources upon which one had to depend were oral rather than written? Surely Paul should be most reliable and Mark next.

But why would Matthew and Luke include stories which were not historically true? One must realize that these men did not think of themselves, any of them, as writing scripture when they were writing. Paul was writing to give direction to the churches which he had helped to establish. Mark was writing to preserve a tradition which needed to be preserved because all of the people who had lived with Jesus were dying and there would soon be no one who had known him alive. Matthew and Luke were writing to supplement that which existed in writing about Jesus, but also with definite and specific purposes of their own. Naturally, after 10 or 20 years of circulation of the book of Mark as the only existing "life of Jesus" one another began to write one he would want to fill in some of the deficiencies of the existing "life". Thus when Matthew and Luke began to write they included stories about the birth of Jesus which probably came into existence after Paul and Mark had written, in order to fill up an obvious gap in the written life of Jesus.

On this basis the birth stories can be seen as theological statements, in which case they are valuable. But they need not and in fact should not be seen as historical, because critical investigation does not support them as historical and because if seen as historical they presuppose belief in a metaphysical system which is no longer acceptable in our time.

The second problem in the life of Jesus is much easier. Once one has realized that he does not have to accept the metaphysical presuppositions of the birth accounts, the story of Jesus in the temple at 12 years of age presents no problem. It is obvious that any child would have been impressed by the temple in Jerusalem, especially on his first visit there. It is no wonder that he took an extended tour of the place. And his questions with the leaders is not so astounding. Doubtless all his life Jesus was a religious person. He, as any normal Jewish boy, would have known much about the Jewish law. With only a little more interest than the average Jewish boy, one could imagine his having stayed in the temple, unaware, as boys often are, that the time for his departure was at hand. The unusual answers which he gave can again be credited to poetic license in dealing with an account several years after the event. The interest in the temple and the law would have been natural for any Jewish boy and especially for one who was interested in his religion.

The ministry of Jesus is the next problem area. What does one do with the fact that Jesus seems to exercise divine power, but in a metaphysical context which is contrary to our own? The phenomenon of psychosomatic medicine aids one greatly here. It is a fact that one can, because of his mental state, cause a physical ailment to develop. This physical ailment can be arrested by general medicine but seldom cured, because the cause is not basically medical but psychological. The real cure in such case is a psychological cure. On this basis almost all of the healings which Jesus performed can be justified. And those in which this cannot be done, one needs to remember that while the Hebrew mind had a great capacity for remembering, it also had a great capacity for exaggeration. Couple this with the time lapse between the events recorded and the time of writing and one has a credibility gap with which he must reckon.

But what about the accounts in which Jesus raises certain individuals from the dead? A careful reading of these accounts will allow one to realize that in all of the incidents except one, that of Lazarus, the people are very recently dead. Accounts exist today of people who have died and been revived. Why could this not have been true then?

The case of Lazarus is different. It is found in the Gospel of John. This gospel is even later than the others in point of time and is entirely different in approach from the other Gospels. It is through and through a theological statement about Jesus. This event of the raising of Lazarus after three days must be seen as a theological statement presupposing the resurrection of Jesus himself. It does not intend to be historical, but theological, just as the birth stories are theological, but not historical.

This raises the issue of Jesus' resurrection. Here again we need to depend upon all of our written accounts and not just some of them. In this case there are several things which must be seen. First, concerning the gospel accounts of the resurrection, let it be remembered that Mark's gospel was the first one written. The resurrection story in Mark is very short and incomplete, containing only the fact that the women found the tomb empty, a young man in a white robe tells them that Jesus has risen, and that they will see him. The oldest manuscripts of the gospel of Mark end at 16:8, omitting the verses which tell of the appearances of Jesus.

The other Gospels do recor events of the appearances of Jesus. Three things of importance should be noted about all of these appearances. First, Jesus does not appear to anyone who had not previously been a close friend or follower. Second, he is not recognizable immediately to any of these close friends or followers when he first appears to them. It is only after he speaks to them that they recognize who he is. Third, this process of his speaking in order for them to recognize him is necessary upon each appearance, not just upon the first appearance. This obviously means that he was not at all like he was before the crucifixion. In the resurrected form his presence in their midst was so different that it took an act of active communication on his part for them to be able to recognize him.

You will remember that Paul's letters were written before any of the other New Testament writings. While Paul says nothing about the birth of Jesus at all, the same is not true concerning the resurrection. In fact, the resurrection is a very frequent theme in Paul's letters. He also records for us an account of the appearance of Jesus to him (I COR. 15). The thing of significance in this account is that he lists the appearance of Jesus to him in the same way as he lists the appearance to the other disciples.

Any student of the New Testament will know from Paul's own letters that he did not get along well with the other apostles, especially on the question of whether one had to submit to the Jewish laws and ceremonies in order to be a Christian (see the letter to the Galatians especially). According to the Book of Acts (1:15-26, esp. 21-22), the role of apostle had to be based upon knowledge of Jesus and of his resurrection. One cannot read the opening of any of Paul's letters without being aware that he claims the office of apostle for himself. And he does so on the basis of the appearance of the resurrected Jesus to him. The book of Acts records the appearance of Jesus to Paul at three different times. On each of these times the thing that is important is that Jesus communicates with Paul rather than appears to him in anything like a bodily form. If the original disciples had had Jesus appear to them in bodily form and Paul had not, why did they not use this as proof of the ineffectiveness of his authority when he caused so much trouble about the Jewish ceremony and legalism controversy? The degree of acceptance of Paul as co-apostle and co-authority with the original disciples indicates that they accepted the appearance of Jesus to Paul as being just as valid as those appearances to themselves. This seems to indicate that the appearances must have been similar. This being true, why not trust Paul's own account of his appearances to him as indicative of the form of the resurrection, giving his closer proximity historically to the events reported, plus the fact that he writes first hand rather than secondhand about the event?

Thus, the metaphysical problems of the resurrection dissipate before a close, full reading of all the accounts of the resurrection, giving precedent to those in closest historical proximity to the events being described.

One further problem remains concerning the events of the life of Jesus, although it is really a by-product rather than an actual event of his life. What does one make of the fact that the apostles preached that the resurrection of Jesus was predicted in scripture and thus is the fulfillment of scripture? This assumption is based upon a view of scripture which also is no longer credible, especially in the area of prophecy. At the present a prophet is seen not as one who predicted events of the long-range future, and to some extent, not generally for the immediate future. Rather a prophet is seen as one who spoke to his own time. Extra biblical studies have shown that, given the conditions existing at the time the prophets lived, they were speaking about specific events related to their own time. They made some predictions about the immediate future, but they would have found incredible the claim that they were predicting hundreds of years ahead the things which would happen, even concerning God's sending a Savior. As was true of the writers of the New Testament, so those of the Old Testament: they did not think of themselves as writing scripture. In fact, for most of them written scripture did not exist until after their time.

Surely this would be true of the writers of the Psalms. The Psalms were composed largely for devotional purposes, either for individuals or for group worship. Yet the largest number of scripture quotations which are used to support the view of Jesus as a divinely predicted Savior come either from the prophets or the Psalms. If in their original intention the writers of this material did not intend to be predicting, especially by divine prompting, the advent of a Savior of men, by what right do we have to prove the divinity of Jesus of Nazareth by using their words to do so?

What then does this look at the original purposes of the writers of both the old and New Testament, the historical sequence of the written sources about Jesus, depending most heavily upon the original sources and those in closest historical proximity to the events described, and the examination of the miracles of Jesus by modern psychological standards leave us?

We now have a man, born of natural circumstances to a Jewish family, with a normal interest in his Jewish religion, who dies and has the claim made for him that he is raised from the dead, but all in metaphysically acceptable concepts.

That is, metaphysical concepts which are valid for today's world and therefore acceptable as having been possible in that day as well.

But what of the claim that this human Jesus of Nazareth was the Son of God? If the traditional proofs of divinity are abolished, can he be in any sense divine, the Son of God and therefore Savior of Man?

III.

Jesus of Nazareth can be seen as divine only if he is first allowed to be seen as human. In the first place, he never makes the claim of divinity for himself. He does refer to himself quite often as Son of Man, but never as Son of God. Son of man is a term which he uses from the book of Daniel in the Old Testament. In the book of Daniel the Son of man was to be one who brings the end of the world, the eschatological end-bringer. By choosing this term by which to refer to himself he repudiates his having any knowledge of a tradition in his lifetime which claimed that he was Son of God by divine decree. If he had, why would he have deliberately chosen another term which did not convey those wonderful facts about this life?

Once one rids himself of the feeling that Jesus' birth must be seen in miraculous terms, the relationship between Jesus and prophecy can be seen clearly. There is no question that Jesus' life and some of the elements of prophecy coincide. This is most obvious in the short passage in the fourth chapter of Luke (Luke 4:16-21). In this passage Jesus announces his intentions for his life to his hometown people. As a means of doing so he reads from the prophet Isaiah. The things he intends to do are: preach the good news to the poor, proclaim release to the captives, recover sight for the blind, set at liberty those who are oppressed. Now remember the things which he did in his ministry and you will recall that these are the things which he did. Jesus not only says he intends to do these things, he does them.

The passage to which he refers here is from the book of the prophet Isaiah who developed the idea of the "suffering servant". There is a great deal of discussion in scholarly circles about these "servant" passages. Some say that the servant was conceived by Isaiah as being an individual who would suffer for the people. Others say that the "servant" was to be the suffering nation of Israel, and that the passages were limited only to Isaiah's comments about the nation of Israel at the time he was writing. Probably both are correct. There are times when Isaiah seems to be talking of an individual and times when he seems to be talking of a collective unit. At any rate, given Jesus' birth under natural conditions, there can be little question that he consciously chose this role of suffering servant as his own, not because it was foreordained by divine decree, but because he saw this as his way of serving his God and Father.

This is consistent with his choice of the term "Son of Man" from Daniel as the term by which he refers to himself. He was convinced that if he assumed the role of deliverer by becoming the suffering servant he would become the end-bringer also. If someone would fulfill this suffering servant role, God would save his people. It is in this context that the phrase from the Gospel of John, "... I lay down my life, that I may take it again. No one takes it from me, but I lay it down of my own accord" (John 10:17b-18a), becomes understandable.

Given today's understanding of the relationship between man and God few people would say that God determines in advance everything that happens to people. He does not predestine a time for us to die. Why would he have done so for Jesus either, especially when we see Jesus as a normal human being? It is only when we are forced to see him as the divine Son of God from the beginning that we are forced to say that God predestined him to death, and therefore make God himself inconsistent. He forced Jesus to die, but he does not force men to die at a certain time in the present. God can be consistent only if Jesus did choose to die; only if he did lay down his own life out of his conscious choice of trying to fulfill the role of suffering servant.

This then is the relationship between Jesus and prophecy. Jesus, as a religious Jew, conscientiously decided for himself to fulfill the role of suffering servant for the nation of Israel, as he discovered the role set forth in Isaiah especially. He chooses for himself the title "Son of Man" from Daniel because he is convinced that in fulfilling the role of suffering servant he will also become the eschatological end-bringer of the book of Daniel.

This view of Jesus and prophecy is consistent with the best understandings of prophecy which are available for us. It allows a Jesus who is consistent with our present understanding of metaphysics. It moves the question of the divinity of Jesus from a miraculously instilled divine nature to an acquired divine nature through conscious choice on the part of one human Jesus of Nazareth.

Remembering that some of the healings of Jesus can be understood in modern psychological and psychosomatic terms so that they can be seen as consistent with our understanding of metaphysics and that others, especially the raising of Lazarus, should be seen as theological rather than historical statements, there is one element of them which must now be considered. This new element becomes especially important in the light of Jesus as having consciously chosen the role of suffering servant and Son of Man.

Recall any "miracle" of the New Testament which you will. Examine it so as to make it fit into our present understanding of metaphysics. When this is finished, one cannot escape the fact that when one who has a need is confronted by Jesus, he has his need met. Quite often what happens is not what the person requested when he came. Quite often Jesus says or does something other than what the asker asked and expected of him. But the simple fact that when Jesus confronts people he helps them cannot be overlooked. Lineup one "miracle" after the other and this is true. Granted, in order to make the events acceptable in our metaphysical system, much of what Jesus does has to be seen as occurring on the psychological level. But how many people do you know today who have the insight into the real needs of people that Jesus had? And how many people do you know who are willing and able to do something which will be helpful to almost everyone with whom he comes into contact?

Simply seen in human terms, Jesus' ability and willingness to help people is unusual. How could he do this? Few people today have known the strength of conscious choice of a religious role with the strength of history and purpose as that role which Jesus chose for himself.

The force of this role which Jesus chose is seen in the fact that it soon becomes distorted into what we now see as the Christian tradition concerning him. The role he chose was one which was existentially related to the life and times in which he lived. Granted, the people in his day had some problems in understanding the new implications and aspects of the role, such as the non—political implications, which Jesus chose. But they had no problem in relating his "fulfilling" of the role to their own religious tradition.

The power of this self-chosen role of Jesus was that it did have a fairly long and venerable tradition which automatically related him to the lives of many of the people once he assumed it. "The medium was the message", to a point... The problem arose for the people when they allowed the medium to become the entire message, and paid no attention to the new content which Jesus brought to it.

But does this make Jesus divine? Here the concept of man is made in the image of God from Genesis will help. Given our metaphysical understanding, this can mean little else than a mental image, and/or an image of will. We are so little versed in matters of the mind that is difficult to say that such a willful and conscious decision based upon such a strong religious tradition would not be able to empower one with what would, under normal conditions, the more than human powers. (That is, we consider normal human powers to be average human powers. Jesus was considered divine by the church because he seemed to perform acts which were more than normal humanly. For a lack of a better area in which to locate the source of power they located it in a power outside our metaphysical system, which led to a distortion of metaphysics.) Jesus' power to help people may have been "divine" only in the sense that he used his "image of God" to better advantage than other people have been willing or able to do.

If we must defend the "divinity" of Jesus, it seems much better to defend his "divinity" on the level of appropriation of the power of the "image of God" in mind and will through conscious choice of a religious and existentially powerful role for his own time, than it does to defend it on the basis of a metaphysical system which is no longer feasible to defend.

Then, what of the resurrection, from the consideration given it above, there can be little question that the resurrection appearances were in essence a matter of communication between the person of Jesus and the closest followers, plus the apostle Paul. In psychic phenomena the matter of communication between the living and the dead is still in a pretty fragmentary state. But there is a good bit of research, especially in England, which seems to substantiate the fact that the presence of dead people can be known and felt by the living (see The Christian Agnostic, Leslie Weatherhead, Abington press, chapters).

There can be little question that something happened to the disciples after the crucifixion. Before the resurrection appearances they were despondent and not greatly changed men. After the appearances they were bold, straightforward men. The same is true of Paul concerning the change. The nature of the change is different. He changes his strenuous efforts from persecution of the church to zeal for the church. But the fact of change remains. There can be little doubt. These people experience something which changed their lives. The thing that is important here is that through a careful reading of the records of the resurrection of Jesus in the New Testament even, the understanding of the event can and should be moved from the area of non-acceptable metaphysical terms to acceptable ones. A physical resurrection cannot and should not be defended, even on the basis of these records. The only resurrection which can be defended is a communicative one.

What view of Jesus, then, does this give us? Rather than the traditional Christian view, Jesus should be seen as a normal Jewish boy, born under normal and natural conditions, who became so impressed by his religious tradition that he takes it upon himself to fulfill a part of that tradition, the suffering servant role of Isaiah, and thereby becomes the eschatological end-bringer of the Son of Man in Daniel. As a result of his conscious choice of these roles he appropriates enough more of the "image of God" which exists for us all that he appears "divine". He manifests his "divinity" in his unusual ability and willingness to see the real needs of people and help them in their real needs when he confronts them. As a result of his efforts in helping (and re-interpreting his religious tradition is a part of his helping) he arouses the anger of the religious leaders of the day. He consciously chooses to die in order to prove the "suffering servant" role as real and effective and effects a communicative resurrection through which he is able to continue to affect the lives of men to the extent that the church grows up around his name. Thus Jesus intended to create the end-time, but created the church instead. The church has inherited his role.

IV.

What, if any, is the value of such a Jesus? In the traditional Christian view, the emphasis is on the miracles rather than on the person of Jesus because these are supposed to prove his divinity. In the view set forth above the emphasis is on the person of Jesus as an historical person, which allows him to be metaphysically acceptable to our time. The traditional Christian view emphasizes miraculous events of his birth, pays little attention to his life and ministry except where the miracles are used to prove his divinity, and presents a miraculous physical resurrection, again bent on proving his divinity. The humanity of Jesus is swallowed up and replaced by an outdated metaphysic bent on improving the divinity, or more than human nature, of Jesus.

What place do each of these elements of Jesus' life play in the view reconstructed above and particularly of what value are they to the life of the church which Jesus inadvertently founded?

First, the birth of Jesus becomes unimportant except when seen in the perspective of the remainder of his life, and then only as it is seen theologically. Therefore, comment about the birth must be reserved until later. Second, the life of Jesus must be seen as the most important aspect of his existence, because it is here that he becomes the Christ, in a historical sense. Three basic points are important in his life.

1. The importance and value of conscious choice as a means of serving God is presented. This is not to say that this consciousness of the need of choosing arises naturally within one. Jesus' choice was made within the context of his religious tradition and with religious training and orientation. But others have had and have that same choice. Jesus saw the importance of choosing the role he chose and did so. The church today must be more aware of the conscious choices which it makes, and encourages its members to make. The conscious choice which one makes will determine the degree to which one becomes a true Christian.

2. The importance of making one's choices in the context of a tradition which is existentially related to the lives of those in whose midst one chooses is emphasized. Too much the church today attempts to preserve and perpetrate an outdated tradition, as it has done with New Testament metaphysics. The life of Jesus reprimands us for such action and recommends to us exactly the opposite course of action.

3. Helping people meet their real needs becomes the major avenue of service in which the church must involve itself. Here again the life of Jesus reprimands the church. We are more content to try to generate a sense of need which we think we are prepared to meet than we are to understand the real needs which the people we confront have, and try to meet them.

Third, the death of Jesus must become more important than it has in the past. This is true because the death of Jesus must be seen in the light of his choosing it rather than of his having been forced into it. When Jesus is allowed to consciously choose death, love abounds in the cross. This truly becomes good news. One loves enough to really choose to die. And the choice of dying is made in the same context as the choice of living – on the context of helping men understand their needs and have them met.

Fourth, the resurrection remains something of a problem area practically, except that when it is seen as a communicative resurrection in becomes metaphysically acceptable for us. It, as the birth, may best be seen theologically. When one communicates with the power of God manifested in the resurrection, he too becomes powerful. It is the communicative power of the resurrection which encourages and enables one to implement the necessary factors of the life of Jesus for oneself.

On the same basis, the birth of Jesus becomes theologically significant. The birth, seen in the perspective of his life, is best summed up by the gospel of John, (the Word became flesh and dwelt among us..." (John 1:14a). The emphasis here is upon the abiding, helping presence of God's power, manifested in the life of conscious choices for meeting the real needs of men and their current existential situation.

This Jesus is historically and metaphysically acceptable. This is the real Jesus of the New Testament. This is who Jesus is.

Notes

Preface

1 Wootton, *The Invention of Science*, 300.
2 Shailer Mathews, *The Growth of the Idea of God*, 220.

Chapter 1

1 Peter L. Berger, *The Sacred Canopy: Elements of a Sociological Theory of Religion*. While Berger did not present this syllogism in his text, the overall content of his text supports the validity of the syllogism.
2 Archaeology, Wikipedia, the free encyclopedia, retrieved 10/3/2019.
3 Sir Leonard Woolley, *Digging Up the Past*.
4 Kramer, *History Begins at Sumer: Thirty-Nine Firsts in Man's Recorded History*; Timeline of human prehistory, Wikipedia, the free encyclopedia, retrieved 10/14/2019.
5 Wallace, 224.
6 Bonner, *The Social Amoeba*; Bowles & Gintis, *A Cooperative Species: Human Reciprocity and Its Evaluation*; Henrich, "Human Cooperation: The Hunter-Gather Puzzle," *Current Biology* 28 (Oct. 8, 2018): R1143–R1163; Nowak, *Super Cooperators: Altruism, Evolution, and Why We Need Each Other to Succeed* (particularly chapter 6).
7 Mathews, *The Growth of the Idea of God*, 34.
8 For example, Smith, Houston, *The World's Religions*.
9 Gilkey, *Maker of Heaven and Earth: The Christian Doctrine of Creation in the Light of Modern Knowledge*, 49–52.
10 Swanson, *The Birth of the Gods: The Origin of Primitive Beliefs*, 66–70.

11 Grubb, *An Unknown People in an Unknown Land*, 111–116.
12 Wallace, 232–244.
13 Wallace, 233.
14 Morowitz, *The Emergence of Everything: How the world became complex*, 161.
15 Morowitz, 167; Timeline of human prehistory, Wikipedia, the free encyclopedia, retrieved 10/14/2019; History of the City, Wikipedia, the free encyclopedia, retrieved 11/2/2019.
16 For an extended discussion of how a complex of cultural advances affect one another, and human thought about them, see Wootton, part 2, 167–247, particularly the discussion of how perspective painting influenced the development of newly forming scientific concepts.
17 Xenophanes, Wikipedia, the free encyclopedia, retrieved 4/13/2020.

Chapter 2

1 Honing, *The Evolving Animal Orchestra: In Search of What Makes Us Musical*,108.
2 Santa Claus; A visit from St. Nicholas, Wikipedia, the free encyclopedia. Retrieved 10/17/2019.
3 "Structural analogy", in Davidson, Scherer, & Goldsmith, (Eds.), *Handbook of Affective Sciences*, particularly, Goldsmith, H. H., Genetics of emotional development, 300–319.
4 Rodgers and Hammerstein, *South Pacific,* Wikipedia, the free encyclopedia. Retrieved 9/25/2019. While the immediate context for this line referenced racial discrimination, the statement is also true for everything we know.
5 Magritte, Wikipedia, the free encyclopedia. Retrieved 9/6/2019.
6 Pipe, Definition of Pipe at Dictionary.com. Retrieved 9/6/2019; *Webster's Seventh New Collegiate Dictionary* (1970);(Based on Webster's Third New International Dictionary)(1961, 1966).
7 Burr, *Social Constructionism*, 4.
8 For an extended discussion of the development of the academic field of epistemology see, Epistemology, Wikipedia, the free encyclopedia, retrieved 9/27/2019.
9 Damasio, *Descartes' Error.*

10 Social Constructionism, Wikipedia, the free encyclopedia, retrieved 9/27/2019.
11 Berger, Peter L., and Luckmann, Thomas. *The Social Construction of Reality.*
12 Elder-vass, *The Reality of Social Construction*; Harris, *What is Constructionism?*; Hjelm, *Social Constructionisms: Approaches to the study of the human world.*

Chapter 3

1 Morowitz, *The Emergence of Everything: How the world became complex*, 24.
2 Carroll, Lewis. *Alice's Adventures in Wonderland.*
3 A popular, colloquial expression, usually expounded in exasperation, at one's behavior that the speaker finds unbelievable; not unlike the feeling many of you have about me for writing this book.
4 Langton, 41.
5 An admonition that I forgot/ignored for about two weeks while trying to figure out how to write this part of the chapter. KISS Principle, Wikipedia, the free encyclopedia, retrieved 11/26/2019.
6 My personal definition, because it reflects a basic description of who we actually are (a gut) (see Collen, 18: "We are, like all animals, an elaborate tube.") and possibly the only behavior (talking) that distinguishes us from other biological entities. See also the section on "orality" at the beginning of Chapter 5.
7 Le Doux; Timeline of the evolutionary history of life, Wikipedia, the free encyclopedia, retrieved 11/22/2019.
8 Wilson, *On Human Nature.*
9 Shubin, Neil. *Your Inner Fish. A journey into the 3.5-billion-year history of the human body.*
10 McEwen, Robert Stanley. *Vertebrate Embryology.* 4th edition. New York: Holt, 1957.
11 When I first read this description of the development of the vertebrate egg, I was so impressed with the concept of motion in the process I had a T-shirt made with the logo, "You were conceived in motion: keep moving"; but that's another book.

12 Gershon, Michael D. *The Second Brain: the scientific basis of gut instinct and a groundbreaking new understanding of nervous disorders of the stomach and intestines.*
13 Gazzaniga, *The Mind's Past,* 27.
14 Hung, Ramsden, & Roe, "Inherent biases in spontaneous cortical dynamics". In Ding, M. & Glanzman, D. L. (Eds.) *The Dynamic Brain: An exploration of neuronal variability and its functional significance.* Oxford: Oxford University Press. 2011, 83–103.
15 Bias, Dictionary.com, retrieved 11/29/2019.
16 Foster & Kreitzman, 141.
17 Bowlby, 285.
18 Hung, Ramsden, & Roe, 83–103.
19 LeDoux, 20.
20 Le Doux, 11.
21 Le Doux, 30.
22 Le Doux, 11.
23 Hirstein,
24 Hirstein, chapter 4.
25 Hirstein, 239–243.
26 *Webster's Seventh New Collegiate Dictionary* (1970).
27 Byrne & Whiten (Eds).
28 Kramer; Code of Ur-Nammu, Wikipedia, the free encyclopedia, retrieved 1/3/20.
29 Believe: *The Random House Dictionary of the English Language.* New York: Random House. 1973.
30 Goldsmith, 300–319
31 Damasio, *Descartes' Error,* chapter 11 especially.
32 Rose
33 Rose, 296.

Chapter 4

1 Wootton, 368.
2 *Random House Dictionary of the English Language, The.*
3 Rose; While, in my view, Rose has an overappreciation of the positive influence of religion, his observations about the social and cultural influence of the invention of agriculture are well presented.

4 Fisher, 285.
5 Flat earth, Wikipedia, the free encyclopedia, retrieved 1/12/2020.
6 Gould.
7 For an exhaustive review of this concept, see Wootton, chapter 4, "Planet Earth." See also, History of the Center of the Universe, Wikipedia, the free encyclopedia, retrieved 1/14/2020.
8 Biology, Wikipedia, the free encyclopedia, retrieved 1/18/2020.
9 Aristotle's biology, Wikipedia, the free encyclopedia, retrieved 1/18/2020.
10 Mind-body problem, Wikipedia, the free encyclopedia, retrieved 1/18/2020. This article contains a short but fairly comprehensive review of several major contributors to the consideration of this issue.
11 Bloodletting, Wikipedia, the free encyclopedia, retrieved 1/18/2020.
12 Humorism, Wikipedia, the free encyclopedia, retrieved 1/18/2020.
13 Silverman, W. (1980), via, "Why fair tests are needed", jameslindlibrary.org, retrieved 1/17/2020.
14 Germ theory of disease, Wikipedia, the free encyclopedia, retrieved 1/19/2020.
15 Gratzer, For an extended discussion, see chapter 2, "The Scurvy Wars."
16 Mukherjee; references, unless otherwise noted, are from this excellent, exhaustive history of cancer.
17 Mukherjee, 38.
18 Mukherjee, 78.
19 Fara; a fascinating and detailed study of beliefs about magnetism and their effects on culture. From the perspective considered in this book, see especially chapter 6, "God's Mysterious Creation: The Divine Attraction of Natural Knowledge."
20 For an extended discussion of the supposed effect of garlic on magnets, see Wootton, 268–70, 274–279.
21 Loadstone, Wikipedia, the free encyclopedia, retrieved 1/20/2020.
22 Code of Ur-Nammu, items 28, 29, Wikipedia, the free encyclopedia, retrieved 1/29/2020.
23 Gazzaniga, *The Ethical Brain,* 124–126.
24 Wallace, 264.

Chapter 5

1 Armstrong, 356.
2 Wallace, 265.
3 Ong, 15.
4 Language, Wikipedia, the free encyclopedia. Retrieved 3/1/2020.
5 Robinson, 1.
6 McLuhan & Fiore, 48.
7 For a cursory introduction to orality, see Orality, Wikipedia, the free encyclopedia. Retrieved 2/11/2020; for a thorough, scholarly treatment of the topic, see Ong, *Orality and Literacy.*
8 Ong, 21; Parry.
9 Lord, 24.
10 All definitions in the following section are from Dictionary.com. I chose this source because it is likely a prominent source for most people currently. However, as the discussion in the text ensues, please recall the third epigraph at the top of the chapter, particularly in relation to the meanings given in dictionary.com and the implications of the meanings in the discussion in the text.
11 Paterson, 4.
12 Signal transduction. Wikipedia, the free encyclopedia. Retrieved 4/3/2020.
13 Damasio, *The Strange Order of Things*, 235–237.
14 Arendt.
15 Arendt, 82.
16 Arendt, 86.
17 Hoebel, *The Law of Primitive Man: A Study in Comparative Legal Dynamics*, 257.
18 Hoebel. *The Law of Primitive Man.*
19 Hoebel, *The Law of Primitive Man,* 4.
20 Hoebel, "Authority in Primitive Societies, 222–3.
21 Hoebel, "Authority in Primitive Societies," 225.
22 Hendel, 16.
23 Freidrich, 34.
24 Freidrich, 37.
25 Hendel, 7.
26 Planning, Wikipedia, the free encyclopedia. Retrieved 4/8/2020.
27 Tool use by animals, Wikipedia, the free encyclopedia, retrieved 4/8/2020. This reference includes an extended discussion of

various species using tools and an extensive bibliography of sources about the topic.

28 Lavars. A video of the action is included in the article.

29 Grandin, Temple, & Johnson, Catherine, 244–248.

30 Hauser, xviii–xix.

31 Hauser, 59.

32 Code of Ur-Nammu, Wikipedia, the free encyclopedia, retrieved 1/3/20.

33 Thales of Miletus, Wikipedia, the free encyclopedia. Retrieved 4/15/2020.

34 Xenophanes, Wikipedia, the free encyclopedia. Retrieved 5/13/2020.

35 Prodicus, Wikipedia, the free encyclopedia. Retrieved 4/15/2020.

36 Democritus, Wikipedia, the free encyclopedia, retrieved 4/13/2020.

37 Pyrrhonism, Wikipedia, the free encyclopedia. Retrieved 4/16/2020.

38 Author: Marcus Tullius Cicero, Wikipedia, the free encyclopedia, retrieved 4/12/2020.

39 Cicero. *The Nature of the Gods; De Natura Deorum,* Wikipedia, the free encyclopedia, retrieved 4/12/2020.

40 Stoicism, Wikipedia, the free encyclopedia, retrieved 4/19/2020.

41 Lucretius, Wikipedia, the free encyclopedia. Retrieved 4/19/2020; Lucretius, *On the Nature of Things; De rerum natura,* Wikipedia, the free encyclopedia, retrieved 2/21/2020.

42 Polis, Wikipedia, the free encyclopedia. Retrieved 4/13/2020.

43 Religion in ancient Rome, Wikipedia, the free encyclopedia. Retrieved 4/13/2020.

44 Eastern Religions, Wikipedia, the free encyclopedia, retrieved 4/19/2020.

45 Confucianism, Wikipedia, the free encyclopedia, retrieved 4/19/2020.

46 Taoism, Wikipedia, the free encyclopedia. Retrieved 4/15/2020.

47 Eastern Religions, Wikipedia, the free encyclopedia, retrieved 4/19/2020.

48 Judaism, Wikipedia, the free encyclopedia, retrieved 4/16/2020.

49 Indigenous religion, Wikipedia, the free encyclopedia, retrieved 4/16/2020.

50 Toffanin.

51 *Catholic Encyclopedia* (1913)/St. Victorinus. Retrieved from https://en.wikisource.org/w/index.php?title=Catholic_Encyclopedia_(1913)/St._Victorinus&oldid=4650404 (Retrieved 4/12/2020).
52 Toffanin, 4.
53 Constantine the Great, Wikipedia, the free encyclopedia, retrieved 4/21/2020.
54 Ecumenical council, Wikipedia, the free encyclopedia, retrieved 4/21/2020.
55 Brown.
56 For an extended summary of modern humanism, see Murry, 25–48.
57 Humanism, Wikipedia, the free encyclopedia, retrieved 4/22/2020.
58 List of secularistic organizations, Wikipedia, the free encyclopedia, retrieved 4/23/2020.
59 American Humanist Association, Wikipedia, the free encyclopedia, retrieved 4/23/2020.
60 Humanist Manifesto, Wikipedia, the free encyclopedia, retrieved 4/22/2020.
61 American Humanist Association, Wikipedia, the free encyclopedia, retrieved 4/23/2020.
62 Hippocratic Oath, Wikipedia, the free encyclopedia, retrieved 4/2/2020.
63 World population, Wikipedia, the free encyclopedia, retrieved 4/24/2020.
64 Religious Composition by Country, 2010–2050. Pew Research Center. retrieved 4/24/2020.
65 Theism, Wikipedia, the free encyclopedia, retrieved 4/24/2020.
66 Pantheism, Wikipedia, the free encyclopedia, retrieved 4/24/2020.
67 Deism, Wikipedia, the free encyclopedia, retrieved 4/24/2020.
68 *Class Clown*. George Carlin. (2009). Available on audio CD.
69 Buckley, *At the Origins of Modern Atheism.*
70 Buckley, *Denying and Disclosing God: The Ambiguous Progress of Modern Atheism.*

Chapter 6

1 Wallace, 270.
2 Damasio, *The Feeling of What Happens: Body and Emotions in the Making of Consciousness*, 315.

3 Nowak, 268.
4 McNeill, 155.
5 Thought experiment, Wikipedia, the free encyclopedia, retrieved 4/29/2020.
6 Prehistoric warfare, Wikipedia, the free encyclopedia. Retrieved 4/7/2020.
7 Kelly, *Warless Societies and the Origin of War;* Kelly, "The Evolution of lethal intergroup violence,", *PNAS,* October 25, 2005, Vol. 102. No. 43, 15294–15298. www.pnas.org/cgi/doi/10.1073/pnas.0505955102. Retrieved 1/12/2020.
8 Azar.
9 Military budget of the United States, Wikipedia, the free encyclopedia (extrapolated by percentage of world amount). Retrieved 4/29/2020.
10 Slavery, Wikipedia, the free encyclopedia. Retrieved 4/30/2020.
11 Crusades, Wikipedia, the free encyclopedia, retrieved 4/30/2020.
12 Nongbri, 157.
13 Early modern period, Wikipedia, the free encyclopedia, retrieved 5/8/2020.
14 Smith, Wilfred Cantwell.
15 Wallace.
16 Ritual, Dictionary.com, retrieved 4/28/2020.
17 Wallace, 224.
18 Teleki.
19 Roman Culture/Roman Religion and Ritual, Wikipedia, the free encyclopedia. Retrieved 5/9/2020.
20 Wallace, 232–3.
21 Rappaport, 25–52.
22 Kauffman.
23 Golden Rule, Wikipedia, the free encyclopedia. Retrieved 5/10/2020.
24 Creed, Dictionary.com, retrieved, 5/11/2020.
25 Murry, 32–33, 37.
26 Pledge of Allegiance, Wikipedia, the free encyclopedia. Retrieved 5/11/2020.
27 Creed (disambiguation), Wikipedia, the free encyclopedia. Retrieved 5/11/2020.
28 American creed, Wikipedia, the free encyclopedia. Retrieved 5/13/2020.

29 McNeill, 152–157.
30 Ochs; Phil Ochs in Concert, Wikipedia, the free encyclopedia. Retrieved 5/13/2020.
31 Damasio, *Looking for Spinoza: Joy, Sorrow, and the Feeling Brain,* 30.
32 Damasio, *The Feeling of What Happens: Body and Emotions in the Making of Consciousness,* 37.

Chapter 7

1 Projections of population growth, Wikipedia, the free encyclopedia. Retrieved 5/14/2020.
2 Genetically modified organism, Wikipedia, the free encyclopedia. Retrieved 5/14/2020.
3 Genetic engineering, Wikipedia, the free encyclopedia. Retrieved 5/16/2020.
4 Cribb.
5 Goodell, *The Water Will Come: Rising Seas, Sinking Cities and the Remaking of the Civilized World.*
6 Goodell, *How to Cool the Planet: Geoengineering and the Ambitious Quest to Fix Earth's Climate.*
7 Crutzen, Paul J., Wikipedia, the free encyclopedia, retrieved 5/16/2020.
8 Gore.
9 Metcalfe & Bergstein.

Appendix A

1 Bateson.

Bibliography

Alexander, Charles N., and Ellen J. Langer, eds. *Higher Stages of Human Development. Perspectives on Adult Growth*. New York/Oxford: Oxford University Press, 1990.

Alexander, C. N., J. L. Davies, C. A. Dixon, M. C. Dillbeck, S. M. Druker, R. M. Oetzel, J. M. Muehlman, and D. W. Orme-Johnson. "Growth of Higher Stages of Consciousness: Maharishi's Vedic Psychology of Human Development." In *Higher Stages of Human Development. Perspectives on Adult Growth*, edited by Charles N. Alexander and Ellen J. Langer, 286–341. New York/Oxford: Oxford University Press, 1990.

American Creed (May 11, 2020). In Wikipedia, https://en.wikipedia.org/wiki/Uniform_Resorce_Locator.

American Humanist Association (2020, April 23). In Wikipedia, https://en.wikipedia.org/wiki/Uniform_Resorce_Locator.

Arendt, Hannah. "What Was Authority?" 81–112. In Carl J. Freidrich,(Ed.). *Authority*. Nomos I. The American Society of Political and Legal Philosophy. Cambridge, MA: Harvard University Press, 1958.

Armstrong, Karen. *A History of God: The 4000-Year Quest of Judaism, Christianity and Islam*. New York: Gramercy Books, 2004.

Author: Marcus Tullius Cicero, (2020, April 12). In Wikipedia, https://en.wikipedia.org/wiki/Uniform_Resorce_Locator.

Azar, Gat. *War in Human Civilization*. New York: Oxford University Press, 2006.

Barlow, Aaron. *The Cult of Individualism: A history of an Enduring American Myth*. Santa Barbara CA: Praeger, 2013.

Bateson, Gregory. *Steps to An Ecology of Mind*. Northvale, NJ: Jason Aronson Inc., 1972, 1978.

Believe: *The Random House Dictionary of the English Language*. New York: Random House, 1973.

Berger, Peter L. *The Sacred Canopy: Elements of a Sociological Theory of Religion*. Garden City New York: Doubleday & Company, Inc., 1967.

Berger, Peter L., & Luckmann, Thomas. *The Social Construction of Reality*. Harmondsworth: Penguin Books, 1971, 1996.

Bias, Dictionary.com, retrieved 11/29/2019.

Bonner, John Tyler. *The Social Amoeba*. Princeton NJ: Princeton University Press, 2009.

Bowlby, John. *Attachment and loss: Vol 2. Separation*. New York: Basic Books, 1973.

Bowles, Samuel & Gintis, Herbert. *A Cooperative Species: Human Reciprocity and its Evaluation*. Princeton NJ: Princeton University Press, 2011.

Brown, Allison. *The Return of Lucretius to Renaissance Florence*. Cambridge MA: Harvard University Press, 2010.

Buckley, Michael J., S. J. *At the Origins of Modern Atheism*. New Haven and London: Yale University Press, 1990.

Buckley, Michael J., S. J. *Denying and Disclosing God: The Ambiguous Progress of Modern Atheism*. New Haven and London: Yale University Press, 2004.

Buckman, Robert. *Can We Be Good Without God? Biology, Behavior, and the Need to Believe.* Amherst, NY: Prometheus Books, 2002.

Burr, V. *Social constructionism. Second edition.* London: Routledge, 2003.

Byrne, Richard W. & Whiten, Andrew (Eds). *Machiavellian Intelligence: Social expertise and the evolution of intellect in monkeys, apes, and humans.* Oxford: Clarendon Press, 1988.

Carroll, Lewis. *Alice's Adventures in Wonderland.* Buffalo, NY: Broadview Press, 1865, 2015.

Catholic Encyclopedia (1913)/St. Victorinus. Retrieved from https://en.wikisource.org/w/index.php?title=Catholic_Encyclopedia_(1913)/St._Victorinus&oldid=4650404 (Retrieved 4/12/2020.

Cicero. *The Nature of the Gods.* (Translated with Introduction and Explanatory Notes by P. G. Walsh.) Oxford: Oxford University Press, 1997.

Code of Ur-Nammu, (2020, January 3). In Wikipedia, https://en.wikipedia.org/wiki/Uniform_Resorce_Locator.

Collen, Alanna. *10% Human: How Your Body's Microbes Hold the Key to Health and Happiness.* New York: Harper, 2015.

Confucianism, (2020, April 19). In Wikipedia, https://en.wikipedia.org/wiki/Uniform_Resorce_Locator.

Constantine the Great, (2020, April 21). In Wikipedia, https://en.wikipedia.org/wiki/Uniform_Resorce_Locator.

Creed, Dictionary.com, retrieved, 5/11/2020.

Cribb, Julian. *The Global Food Crisis and What We Can Do to Avoid It.* Berkley: University of California Press, 2010.

Crusades, (2020, May 30). In Wikipedia, https://en.wikipedia.org/wiki/Uniform_Resorce_Locator.

Crutzen, Paul J., (2020, May 16). In Wikipedia, https://en.wikipedia.org/wiki/Uniform_Resorce_Locator.

Damasio, Antonio R. *Descartes' Error: Emotion, Reason and the Human Brain.* New York: G. P. Putman's Sons, 1994.

Damasio, Antonio R. *The Feeling of What Happens: Body and Emotions in the Making of Consciousness.* New York: Harcourt Brace & Company, 1999.

Damasio, Antonio R. *Looking for Spinoza: Joy, Sorrow, and the Feeling Brain.* New York: Harcourt, Inc., 2003.

Damasio, Antonio R. *Self Comes to Mind. Constructing the Conscious Brain.* New York: Pantheon Books, 2010.

Damasio, Antonio R. *The Strange Order of Things.* New York: Vintage Books, 2018.

de Botton, Alain. *Religion for Atheists: A Non-believer's Guide to the Uses of Religion.* New York: Pantheon Books, 2012.

Deism, (2020, April 24). In Wikipedia, https://en.wikipedia.org/wiki/Uniform_Resorce_Locator.

Democritus,(2020, April 13). In Wikipedia, https://en.wikipedia.org/wiki/Uniform_Resorce_Locator.

De Natura Deorum, (2020, April 12). In Wikipedia, https://en.wikipedia.org/wiki/Uniform_Resorce_Locator.

De rerum natura, (2020, February 21). In Wikipedia, https://en.wikipedia.org/wiki/Uniform_Resorce_Locator.

Diagoras of Melos,(2020, April 13). In Wikipedia, https://en.wikipedia.org/wiki/Uniform_Resorce_Locator.

Dictionary.com, (Collins English Dictionary-Complete and Unabridged 2012 Digital Edition ((Copyright)) William Collins Sons & Co., LTD. 1979, 1986 ((Copyright)) Harper Colling Publishers 1998, 2000, 2003, 2005, 2006, 2007, 2009, 2012., retrieved 3/21/2020).

Ding, M. & Glanzman, D. L. (Eds.). *The Dynamic Brain: An exploration of neuronal variability and its functional significance.* Oxford: Oxford University Press, 2011.

Early modern period,(2020, May 8). In Wikipedia, https://en.wikipedia.org/wiki/Uniform_Resorce_Locator.

Eastern Religions, (2020, April 19). In Wikipedia, https://en.wikipedia.org/wiki/Uniform_Resorce_Locator.

Ecumenical council, (2020, April 21). In Wikipedia, https://en.wikipedia.org/wiki/Uniform_Resorce_Locator.

Elder-vass, Dave. *The Reality of Social Construction.* Cambridge: Cambridge University Press, 2012.

Epistemology, (2019, September 27). In Wikipedia, https://en.wikipedia.org/wiki/Uniform_Resorce_Locator.

Fara, Patricia. *Sympathetic Attractions: Magnetic Practices, Beliefs, and Symbolism in Eighteenth Century England.* Princeton, NJ: Princeton University Press, 1996.

Fisher, Helen E. *Anatomy of Love. The Natural History of Monogamy, Adultery, and Divorce.* New York: W. W. Norton and Company, 1992.

Foley, John Miles. What's in A Sign? In, Mackay, E. Anne (Ed.). *Signs of Orality: The Oral Tradition and Its Influence in the Greek and Roman World.* Leiden, Boston, Koln: Brill, 1999.

Foster, R. G. & Kreitzman, L. *Seasons of Life: the biological rhythms that enable living things to thrive and survive.* New Haven: Yale University Press, 2009.

Fowler, Jeanannc. *Humanism: Beliefs and Practices.* Brighton: Sussex Academic Press, 1999.

Freidrich, Carl J. (Ed.). *Authority.* Nomos I. The American Society of Political and Legal Philosophy. Cambridge, MA.: Harvard University Press, 1958.

Gat, Azar. *War in Human Civilization.* Oxford: New York: Oxford University Press, 2006.

Gazzaniga, Michael S. *The Mind's Past.* Berkeley: University of California Press, 1998.

Gazzaniga, Michael S. *The Ethical Brain.* New York/Washington, DC: Dana Press, 2005.

Genetically modified organism, (2020, May 14). In Wikipedia, https://en.wikipedia.org/wiki/Uniform Resorce Locator.

Gershon, Michael D. *The Second Brain: the scientific basis of gut instinct and a groundbreaking new understanding of nervous disorders of the stomach and intestines.* New York: Harper Collins Publishers, 1998.

Gilkey, Langdon. *Maker of Heaven and Earth: The Christian Doctrine of Creation in the Light of Modern Knowledge.* New York: Doubleday, 1959, 1985.

Goldsmith, H. H. Genetics of emotional development, pp. 300–319, In Davidson, R. J., Scherer, K. R. & Goldsmith, H. H. (Eds.). *Handbook of Affective Sciences.* Oxford: Oxford University Press, 2003.

Goodell, Jeff. *How to Cool the Planet: Geoengineering and the Ambitious Quest to Fix Earth's Climate.* New York: Houghton Mifflin, Harcourt Publishing Co, 2010.

Goodell, Jeff. *The Water Will Come: Rising Seas, Sinking Cities and the Remaking of the Civilized World.* New York: Little, Brown and Company, 2017.

Gore, Al. *an inconvenient truth: The crisis of global warming.* New York: Rodale, Inc., 2006.

Gould, Stephen J. "The late birth of a flat earth." In *Dinosaur in a Haystack: Reflections in Natural History.* New York: Harmony Books. (1995).

Grandin, Temple,& Johnson, Catherine. *Animals in Translation: Using the Mysteries of Autism to Decode Animal Behavior.* Orlando, etc.: A Harvest Book-Harcourt, Inc., 2006.

Gratzer, Walter. *Terrors of the Table: The Curious History of Nutrition*. Oxford: Oxford University Press, 2005.

Grubb, W. Barbroke. *An Unknown People in an Unknown Land*. H. T. Morrey Jones, M. A., editor. Philadelphia: J. B. Lippincott Company, 1911.

Hamer, Dean. *The God Gene: How Faith Is Hardwired into Our Genes*. New York: Doubleday, 2004.

Harris, Scott R. *What is Constructionism?* Bolder: Lynne Rienner Publishers, 2010.

Hauser, Marc D. *Wild Minds: What Animals Really Think*. New York: Henry Holt and Company, 2000.

Hecht, Jenifer Michael. *Doubt: A History. The great doubters and their legacy of innovation, from Socrates and Jesus to Thomas Jefferson and Emily Dickinson*. New York: Harper San Francisco, 2003.

Hendel, Charles W. "An Explanation of the Nature of Authority", 3–27. In Freidrich, Carl J. (Ed.). *Authority*. Nomos I. The American Society of Political and Legal Philosophy. Cambridge, MA.: Harvard University Press, 1958.

Henrich, Joseph. Oct 8, 2018. Human Cooperation: The Hunter-Gather Puzzle. *Current Biology 28*, R1143–R1163.

Hippocratic Oath, (2020, April 2). In Wikipedia, https://en.wikipedia.org/wiki/Uniform_Resorce_Locator.

Hirstein, William. *Brain Fiction: Self-Deception and the Riddle of Confabulation*. Cambridge, MA: The MIT Press, 2005.

History of the City, (2019, November 2). In Wikipedia, https://en.wikipedia.org/wiki/Uniform_Resorce_Locator.

Hjelm, Titus. *Social Constructionisms: Approaches to the study of the human world*. UK: Palgrave Macmillan, 2014.

Hoebel, E. Adamson. *The Law of Primitive Man. A Study in Comparative Legal Dynamics*. Cambridge, MA: Harvard University Press, 1954.

Hoebel, Adamson. "Authority in Primitive Societies, 222–234." In Freidrich, Carl J. (Ed.). *Authority*. Nomos I. The American Society of Political and Legal Philosophy. Cambridge, MA: Harvard University Press, 1958.

Holland, John H. *Signals and Boundaries: Building Blocks for Complex Adaptive Systems*. Cambridge, MA: the MIT Press, 2014.

Honing, Henkjan. *The Evolving Animal Orchestra. In Search of What Makes Us Musical*. (translated by Sherry Macdonald). Cambridge MA.: The MIT Press, 2019.

Humanism, (2020, April 22). In Wikipedia, https://en.wikipedia.org/wiki/Uniform_Resorce_Locator.

Humanist Manifesto, (2020, April 22). In Wikipedia, https://en.wikipedia.org/wiki/Uniform_Resorce_Locator.

Hung, C. P., Ramsden, B. M., & Roe, A. W. "Inherent biases in spontaneous cortical dynamics". In Ding, M. & Glanzman, D. L. (Eds.). *The Dynamic Brain: An exploration of neuronal variability and its functional significance*. Oxford: Oxford University Press, 2011.

Indigenous religion, (2020, April 16). In Wikipedia, https://en.wikipedia.org/wiki/Uniform_Resorce_Locator.

Judaism, (2020, April 16). In Wikipedia, https://en.wikipedia.org/wiki/Uniform_Resorce_Locator.

Kauffman, Stuart A. *The Origins of Order: Self Organization and Selection in Evolution*. New York: Oxford University Press, 1993.

Kelly Raymond. C. *Warless Societies and the Origin of War*. Ann Arbor: University of Michigan Press, 2000.

Kelly, Raymond C. The evolution of lethal intergroup violence. *PNAS*. October 25, 2005, Vol. 102, No. 43, 15294–15298. www.pnas.org/cgi/doi/10.1073/pnas.0505955102.

KISS Principle, (2019, November 26). In Wikipedia, https://en.wikipedia.org/wiki/Uniform_Resorce_Locator.

Kohlberg, Lawrence, Ryncarz, Robert A. "Beyond Justice Reasoning: Moral Development and Consideration of a Seventh Stage", 191–207. In Alexander, Charles N., Langer, Ellen J. (Eds.). *Higher Stages of Human Development: Perspectives on Adult Growth*. New York/Oxford: Oxford University Press, 1990.

Kramer, Samuel Noah. *History Begins at Sumer: thirty-nine firsts in man's recorded history*. Philadelphia: University of Pennsylvania Press. (1981).

Langton, Christopher G. "Artificial Life." In Langton, Christopher G. (Ed.) *Artificial Life. The proceedings of an interdisciplinary workshop on the synthesis and simulation of living systems*. Held September, 1987 in Los Alamos, New Mexico. Volume VI, Santa Fe Institute Studies in the Sciences of complexity. Reading, MA: Addison-Wesley Publishing Company, 1989.

Lavars, Nick. "Scientists witness crows building tools from various parts for the first time." *New Atlas*. October 26, 2018. https://newatlas.com.

LeDoux, Joseph. *The Deep History of Ourselves: The four-billion-year-story of how we got our conscious brains*. New York: Viking, 2019.

Lord, Albert. B. *The Singer of Tales:* Harvard Studies in Comparative Literature. Cambridge, MA: Harvard University Press, 1960.

Lucretius. *On the Nature of Things*. (Translated by W. Hannaford Brown, M. A.) New Brunswick: Rutgers University Press, 1950. (Original work published first century BCE.)

Lucretius, 2020, April 19). In Wikipedia, https://en.wikipedia.org/wiki/Uniform_Resorce_Locator.

MacGregor, Neil. *A History of the World in 100 Objects.* London: Penguin, 2010.

Magritte, (2019, September 6). In Wikipedia, https://en.wikipedia.org/wiki/Uniform_Resorce_Locator.

Matthews, Shailer. *The Growth of the Idea of God.* New York: Macmillan, 1931.

McEwen, Robert Stanley. *Vertebrate Embryology.* 4th edition. New York: Holt, 1957.

McLuhan, Marshall & Fiore, Quentin. *The Medium is the Massage.* New York: Bantam Books, 1967.

McNeill, William H. *Keeping Together In Time. Dance and Drill in Human History.* Cambridge, MA: Harvard University Press, 1995.

Metcalfe, Jane & Bergstein, Brian. *Neo.Life: 25 Visions for the Future of Our Species.* Berkley: Neo.Life, Inc, 2019.

Military budget of the United States,(2020, April 29). In Wikipedia, https://en.wikipedia.org/wiki/Uniform_Resorce_Locator.

Montaigne, Michael de. *The Essays of Montaigne.* (Translated from the French by E. J. Trechmann). New York: Random House: The Modern Library, 1946.

Morowitz, Harold J. *The Emergence of Everything: How the world became complex.* New York: Oxford University Press, 2002.

Mukherjee, Siddhartha. *The Emperor of all Maladies.* New York: Scribner, 2010.

Murry, William R. *Reason and Reverence: Religious Humanism for the 21st Century.* Boston: Skinner House Books, 2007.

Nongbri, Brent. *Before Religion: A History of a Modern Concept.* New Haven: Yale University Press, 2013.

Nowak, Martin A.(with Roger Highfield). *Super Cooperators: Altruism, Evolution, and Why We Need Each Other to Succeed.* New York: Free Press, 2011.

Ochs, Phil. (1965–66). *Phil Ochs in Concert.* "When I'm Gone". Boston & New York: Elektra.

Ong, Walter J. *Orality and Literacy: The Technologizing of the Word.* (With additional chapters by John Henry). 30th Anniversary Edition. Routledge: London and New York, 2002.

Orality, (2020, February 11). In Wikipedia, https://en.wikipedia.org/wiki/Uniform Resorce Locator.

Panksepp, Jaak. *Affective Neuroscience: The Foundations of Human and Animal Emotions.* New York: Oxford University Press, 1998.

Panksepp, Jaak. Toward a cross-species understanding of empathy. *Trends in Neuroscience.* 2013 August; 36(8): doi:10.1016/j.tins.2013.04.009.

Pantheism, (2020, April 24). In Wikipedia, https://en.wikipedia.org/wiki/Uniform Resorce Locator.

Parry, Milman. *The Making of Homeric Verse.* (English Translation): Parry, Adam (Ed.). Oxford: Clarendon Press, 1971.

Paterson, Mark. *The Senses of Touch. Haptics, Affects and Technologies.* Oxford, New York: Berg, 2007.

Phil Ochs in Concert, (2020, May 13). In Wikipedia, https://en.wikipedia.org/wiki/Uniform Resorce Locator.

Pipe. Definition of Pipe at Dictionary.com. Retrieved 9/6/2019.

Pledge of Allegiance, Wikipedia,(2020, May 11). In Wikipedia, https://en.wikipedia.org/wiki/Uniform Resorce Locator.

Polis, Wikipedia,(2020, April 13). In Wikipedia, https://en.wikipedia.org/wiki/Uniform Resorce Locator.

Prehistoric warfare, (2020, April 7). In Wikipedia, https://en.wikipedia.org/wiki/Uniform Resorce Locator.

Prodicus, (2020, April 13). In Wikipedia, https://en.wikipedia.org/wiki/Uniform Resorce Locator.

Projections of population growth,(2020, May 14). In Wikipedia, https://en.wikipedia.org/wiki/Uniform Resorce Locator.

Pyrrhonism, (2020, April 16). In Wikipedia, https://en.wikipedia.org/wiki/Uniform Resorce Locator.

Pythagoras, (2020, April 13). In Wikipedia, https://en.wikipedia.org/wiki/Uniform Resorce Locator.

Random House Dictionary of the English Language, The. The Unabridged Edition. Stein, Jess, Editor in Chief. New York: Random House, 1973.

Rappaport, Roy A. *Ritual and Religion in the Making of Humanity.* Cambridge: Cambridge University Press, 1999.

Religion in ancient Rome, (2020, April 13). In Wikipedia, https://en.wikipedia.org/wiki/Uniform Resorce Locator.

Religious Composition by Country, 2010–2050. Pew Research Center. retrieved 4/24/2020.

Rite, Dictionary.com, retrieved 4/28/2020.

Ritual, Dictionary.com, retrieved 4/28/2020.

Robinson, Andrew. *Writing and Script. A Very Short Introduction.* Oxford: Oxford University Press, 2009.

Rodgers and Hammerstein. *South Pacific.* (1949). (2019, September 25) In Wikipedia, https://en.wikipedia.org/wiki/Uniform Resorce Locator.

Santa Claus; A visit from St. Nicholas,(2019, October 17). In Wikipedia, https://en.wikipedia.org/wiki/Uniform Resorce Locator.

Secularistic organizations, List of, (2020, April 23,). In Wikipedia, https://en.wikipedia.org/wiki/Uniform Resorce Locator.

Shubin, Neil. *Your Inner Fish. A journey into the 3.5-billion-year history of the human body.* New York: Vintage Books, (2009) (2008).

Signal transduction.(2020, April 3,). In Wikipedia, https://en.wikipedia.org/wiki/Uniform Resorce Locator.
Smith, Houston. *The World's Religions.* New York: Harper Collins, 1958, 1986, 1991.
Smith, Wilfred Cantwell. *The Meaning and End of Religion.* Minneapolis: Fortress Press, 1991, 1962, 1963.
Social Constructionism, (2019, September 27,). In Wikipedia, https://en.wikipedia.org/wiki/Uniform Resorce Locator.
Somatosensory system. (2020 April, 3). In Wikipedia, https://en.wikipedia.org/wiki/Uniform Resorce Locator.
Stoicism, Wikipedia,(2020, April 19). In Wikipedia, https://en.wikipedia.org/wiki/Uniform Resorce Locator.
"Structural analogy", Davidson, R. J., Scherer, K. R. & Goldsmith, H. H. (Eds.). *Handbook of Affective Sciences.* Oxford: Oxford University Press, 2003), particularly, Goldsmith, H. H., Genetics of emotional development, (pp. 300–319).
Taoism, (2020, April 15). In Wikipedia, https://en.wikipedia.org/wiki/Uniform Resorce Locator.
Teleki, Geza. *The Predatory Behavior of Wild Chimpanzees.* Lewisburg: Bucknell University Press, 1973.
Thales of Miletus, (2020, April 15). In Wikipedia, https://en.wikipedia.org/wiki/Uniform Resorce Locator.
Thought experiment, (2020, April 29). In Wikipedia, https://en.wikipedia.org/wiki/Uniform Resorce Locator.
Throckmorton, Burton H., Jr. (Ed.). *Gospel Parallels. A Synopsis of the First Three Gospels.* New York: Thomas Nelson & Sons, 1949, 1957.
Timeline of human prehistory, (2019, October 14) In Wikipedia, https://en.wikipedia.org/wiki/Uniform Resorce Locator.

Timeline of the evolutionary history of life, (2019, November 22). In Wikipedia, https://en.wikipedia.org/wiki/Uniform_Resorce_Locator.

Toffanin, Giuseppe. (English translation, Foreword and Augmented Bibliography by Elio Gianturco). *History of Humanism*. New York: Las Americas Publishing Co, 1954.

Tool use by animals, (2020 April 8). In Wikipedia, https://en.wikipedia.org/wiki/Uniform_Resorce_Locator.

Wallace, Anthony F. C. *Religion: An Anthropological View*. New York: Random House, 1966.

Walsh, P. G. Introduction and Explanatory Notes. In *Cicero. The Nature of the Gods*. Oxford: Oxford University Press, 1997. (Originally published first century BCE).

Webster's Seventh New Collegiate Dictionary, 1970; (Based on Webster's Third New International Dictionary), 1961, 1966.

Wilson, E. O., *On Human Nature*. Cambridge: Harvard University Press. 1978.

Woolley, Sir Leonard. *Digging Up the Past*. London: Ernest Benn Limited, 1930; Totowa NJ: Rowman and Littlefield, 1973.

Wootton, David. *The Invention of Science*. New York: Harper, 2015.

World population, (2020, April 24). In Wikipedia, https://en.wikipedia.org/wiki/Uniform_Resorce_Locator.

Xenophanes, (2020, May 13). In Wikipedia, https://en.wikipedia.org/wiki/Uniform_Resorce_Locator.

www.ingramcontent.com/pod-product-compliance
Lightning Source LLC
Chambersburg PA
CBHW020900310526
45786CB00018B/487

* 9 7 8 1 4 8 0 8 9 8 6 9 1 *